HAUNTED
PEAK DISTICT

JILL ARMITAGE

First published 2009

The History Press
The Mill, Brimscombe Port
Stroud, Gloucestershire, GL5 2QG
www.thehistorypress.co.uk

British Library Cataloguing in Publication Data.
A catalogue record for this book is available from the British Library.

ISBN 978 0 7524 5122 0

Typesetting and origination by The History Press
Printed in Great Britain

HAUNTED
PEAK DISTRICT

CONTENTS

Introduction   7

1.   Unexplained Phenomena in this Bleak and Pleasant Land   11
2.   Idols, Heathen Gods and Nature Spirits   41
3.   Road and Rail Frights   73
4.   Beasts, Bones and Odours   99

INTRODUCTION

The hills and valleys of the Peak District have always been fertile grounds for strange observations and happenings. For centuries, the level of extraordinary phenomena reported from the bleak moors and valley hamlets has been far beyond that experienced virtually anywhere else in the Northern Hemisphere. Scratch the surface of the heather-covered moorlands and you'll find supernatural stories from the Dark Ages, because the Peak District is a place where ancient customs and traditions have been retained alongside old beliefs and superstitions. It's a place of living legends that are eroded as slowly as the landscape itself.

The Peak District covers the whole of the west side of Derbyshire and spills over into Staffordshire, Cheshire and West Yorkshire, but the name itself is a misnomer. There is no single gigantic mountain peak where climbers struggle to reach the summit, despite the fact that at times Kinder Scout (636m) and Bleaklow (628m) put on a passable impression of authentic Alpine conditions. The name actually comes from the old English word *peac* which, in the tenth century, meant hill or knoll. The tribes who inhabited the region at this time were known as the 'Pecsaetan' or 'Peak Dwellers' and the area retains a long tradition of lead mining and hill farming.

More than 20 million visitors enjoy the Peak District splendour every year but within the 555 miles² (1,437km²) there are two distinct areas, the White Peak and the Dark Peak. The White Peak takes its name from the rolling limestone dales of the south with their lush lowlands and wooded slopes. This is an area of steep-sided, limestone gorges and bright-green fields criss-crossed by dry stone walls. It's dotted with villages that manage to retain their old-world atmosphere alongside modern amenities.

In contrast, the gritstone of the Dark Peak to the north with its remote, mysterious hills has a rugged, austere beauty. There is something particularly eerie about those featureless, lonely landscapes where the hazy horizon seems to stretch into eternity, and sounds echo from miles around. These windswept moorlands in less favourable weather can be very inhospitable, despite being surrounded by some of the largest industrial conurbations and sandwiched between two of the North's largest cities, Manchester and Sheffield. This is a remote highland region and a number of people who have ventured onto these desolate hills have reported a brooding, elemental presence and a chilling silence. A strange noise or an indefinable shape looming out of a cloudy mist can set the imagination running riot. Could it be a demonic beast or an alien spaceship? People report hearing the marching feet of a legion of Roman

The Peak District is a place where ancient customs and traditions have been retained. A spinner demonstrates at Chatsworth Game Fair, 2008.

soldiers along the lonely moorland expanse of Bleaklow and should you look up you may see phantom bombers flying silently across the sky as they did sixty years ago.

Dark country lanes and moorland roads harbour a multitude of supernatural horrors. Headless horsemen, ghostly carriages and phantom motor vehicles patrol lonely highways, and beware of phantom hitch-hikers and crossroads haunted by a host of spectres, witches and boggarts. Stories of the mysterious and supernatural still continue to fascinate and perplex us, and here in the Peak District these tales are vividly recounted as if they happened yesterday. Some did because many of the obscure elements within ancient legends still recur in the haunting stories of today.

This is my sixth paranormal book and I am still finding more stories, so it is inevitable that research also uncovers some interesting additions. In *Haunted Derbyshire* I relayed how Labour MP Roy Hattersley had bought Church Lady House, a period property in Great Longstone, which also had a ghost. Since then I have found out that the ghost actually gave the house its unusual name. Apparently, this ghostly apparition was often seen by the children of a previous family, yet remained invisible to the adults. The children would casually announce that they had just seen 'the church lady' going to wash her hands in the corner of an adjacent room, presumably a former kitchen. The parents asked why the children called her 'the church lady' and were told that their phantom guest was always dressed in sombre black as if she were about to attend church. The name stuck and the family renamed their home Church Lady House.

While researching, I spoke to many people and witnessed some bizarre incidents. A guide at one of the Peak District Tourist Information Centres felt a draught around his feet and, looking down, realized that his shoelaces were undone. He bent down to retie them but within minutes they were undone again. I watched in fascination as he retied them yet again, using a double knot. It's those kind of incidents that confirm that in the Peak District the supernatural is not stranded in the past, it's all around us right here, right now.

Jill Armitage, 2009

one

UNEXPLAINED PHENOMENA IN THIS BLEAK AND PLEASANT LAND

The Hills are Alive with the Sound of Music

Every year, 20 million people visit the Peak District and many walk the 1,600 miles of footpaths there, but this freedom to roam was only made possible by a band of intrepid walkers who in 1894 formed the Peak District and Northern Counties Footpaths Society, one of the oldest in Britain. Understandably landowners considered this a gross intrusion on their property and were adamantly against it, even going so far as to instruct their gamekeepers to shoot any trespasses. As a protest, in 1932, 500 ramblers held a mass trespass on Kinder Scout and despite five ramblers being arrested and gaoled, overall it was a peaceful protest. This united show of strength, which ended with community singing, contributed to the opening of a large area of Kinder Scout and in 1951 the opening of the first National Park in Britain.

The Peak District National Park still provides an enjoyable summer walking spot, but in less favourable weather this wild and barren place can be very inhospitable. As the wind whistles across the moors it is easy to imagine you can almost hear other, more subtle sounds, but possibly the most bizarre occurrence is the sound of singing.

On the summit of Kinder Scout.

The mass trespass that took place in 1932.

Ramblers continue to report hearing both *The Red Flag* and *The Internationale* sung by what has been described as a male-voice choir. These are not the pop songs of today that are being overheard from the player of some antisocial visitor. They might come from isolated farmsteads or domestic dwellings but as these are few and far between it's hardly likely. What makes this so strange is that people always report hearing the same songs sung with rousing gusto, so it's not surprising to find that this is exactly what happened on that mass trespass back in 1932. Most people now have no recollection of this event or the singing. The people who hear it have no idea that this is an action replay, a repeat performance, an echo that has been absorbed into the rocks of Kinder Scout and is still recurring after more than seventy years.

The Lost Lad and His Dog

The heather-covered moorland scenery of the Dark Peak has a strange and persistently eerie atmosphere, particularly in areas where there are poignant reminders of human catastrophe. Many people have tragically lost their lives after being caught in the open by the severe weather, which can descend suddenly and without warning.

Abraham Lowe, a thirteen-year-old shepherd boy and his faithful dog set out from their hill farm near the village of Derwent, in the Pennines, to bring the family's flock of sheep in from the moorland tops to the sheltered farm in the valley below. Near Black Tor on Derwent Edge, he was caught by the mist that swirled around making him disorientated, and as the snow blanketed the moors, he crawled under a rock for shelter but not before he had scratched the words LOST LAD on the stone.

A lone walker at the beginning of the 270-mile Pennine Way.

Three months passed before a shepherd passed the spot and the remains of Abraham and his faithful dog were found huddled under the rock. Ever since, every shepherd that passes the spot has left a stone on the cairn.

At mid-winter when snow is threatening, farmers, shepherds and hikers all claimed to have caught fleeting glimpses of Abraham and his dog high on Derwent Edge. People who have seen them say they look so real, they have actually called out a greeting but have received no response. But perhaps what is most distressing is the wailing voice. Those who have heard it and searched in vain have tried to reason that it is a bird or animal in pain, but most are convinced that it is a lost child crying 'Momma'.

An abandoned millstone on the snowy Stanage Edge.

The Bells under the Water

Another sound that is often reported in this area is the ringing of church bells. You might imagine this sound could be carried across the valley from any small Peakland church, but you'd be wrong. These bells come from the church in the village of Derwent Woodland which disappeared in 1945 when the Lady Bower reservoir was created. The spire was left and dedicated to the people, but when the water level was low the ruins of the spire would protrude above the water and people climbed it. This was considered dangerous and so the spire was blown up and now all that can be heard is ghostly bells ringing under the water.

Only the church bell tower was left standing, but the sound of ghostly bells are still heard ringing from under the water.

Derwent Church was submerged under the reservoir but when the water level was dangerously low, the ruins re-emerged.

Part of the chancel column from Derwent Church, now in the Dambusters Museum.

Hammering in the Posts

Stories of supernatural experiences don't have to be from somewhere in the dim and distant past. In the 1990s, a young couple rented a seventeenth-century Peak District cottage at a peppercorn rent on condition that they tamed the untended garden. Firstly, they erected a fence to mark the boundary. It was nothing substantial, just stakes hammered into the ground with a few strands of wire between. Knocking the stakes into the stony ground with a small sledgehammer was the most difficult part, but they persevered. A few months later while tending the garden, they paused to listen because from somewhere came the sound of hammering. It could not have been a distant echo as it was too loud. Rather puzzled they moved around the garden and eventually realised that the noise came from their recently erected posts. There was nothing there to explain the noise, but it was the same rhythm and timing as when they had hammered the posts in place. Somehow, those earlier sounds were being replayed.

The Gabriel Hounds

Throughout the country there are the tales of packs of spectral hunting hounds that supposedly glide through the sky on wild, stormy nights searching for lost souls. In north Derbyshire and the Peak District these are known as the Rach Hounds or Gabriel Hounds. They are heard but rarely seen and their howling is said to be an omen of death or disaster. The sounds of their howls decrease as they approach and settle near a person, then once they have marked their victim, they move swiftly away and the sound begins to increase until the horrific howls are petrifying. Terrified dogs and cats apparently run for miles to get away from these spectral hounds.

The prophetic ability of these hounds was widely accepted, but there's a romantic story in the Peak District of how this widespread belief served a useful purpose in thwarting the intentions of an unacceptable suitor. (See also *Romantic Haunts of Derbyshire* by this author.)

It's understandable that we should look for rational explanations for all these sounds. The babble of the brook can suggest ghostly voices engaged in excited conversation; a veteran of that mass trespass could be re-enacting events with his ipod, despite the fact that he'd now be an octogenarian and unlikely to be capable of a repeat performance. The cry of a bird may be the soulful cry of a lost lad; the sound of bells, and the hammering could carry on the still air, the Gabriel Hounds could be geese. But people who have heard the sounds are unconvinced.

The tranquil valley from Monsal Head.

Froggat Edge.

Phantom Fighters

There are other sounds that can't be explained away quite so easily and one of these is the sound and vibration of marching feet. This is an action replay that dates back to the year AD 80 when Julius Agricola the Roman General, having defeated the Cornavii tribe, advanced up the north-east horn of Cheshire to attack the Peak dwellers who were part of the Kingdom of the Brigantines. He ordered them to surrender, a suggestion that was met with a defiant refusal from the haughty Celts. They preferred death in battle to slavery beneath the yoke of Rome.

People have been terrified by the ghostly appearance of Roman soldiers.

The highly disciplined Roman force met the Celts who had mustered their forces on Combes Edge overlooking Glossop, but the untrained hoards were no match for the Romans. Hundreds of Britains, many of them local lead miners, horse-breeders and farmers, were massacred by the well-armed Roman army on Ludworth Moor. The dead were buried and the victorious Romans erected an altar to victory. It is said that at certain times of the year when the moonlight falls on Combes Rocks, the ghosts of ancient warriors waving their phantom axes can still be seen.

Four climbers were able to describe the long, curved shields and the curious helmets of the ghostly Roman legionnaires.

But what of those marching feet that are still heard in the area, particularly on the lonely moorland expanses? It's probably because the Romans remained in the area for over 300 years. They appreciated the warm, curative waters of Buxton and Stoney Middleton and as the Peak District has always been rich in lead, in order to benefit from this, the Romans decided to settle here. The garrison was probably controlled initially from the headquarters of the xxth legion Valeria Victix at Chester but soon they had built forts at Melandra in Glossop and Brough-on-Noe near Bradwell which the Romans called Navio. Linking these two was a lonely road cut through some of the most inhospitable moorland expanses in the Dark Peak, the areas where the sound of those marching feet are still heard today.

In Buxton Museum is a Roman milestone found in 1862 at Silverlands, Buxton, the only known example in Derbyshire. It is inscribed, 'TRIB POT COS II P P A NAVIONE M P XI' which translates, 'with tribunician power, twice consul, father of this country, from Navio II miles.' (The name of the person with the tribunician power is obviously missing.)

Large quantities of lead were mined throughout the Peak district, but lead ore often contained large quantities of silver, so the Peak lead mines would have come under the direct supervision of the Imperial Treasury of Rome. Unfortunately Derbyshire lead contained very little silver which must have been a great disappointment to the treasury officials who quickly leased the mine to civil contractors who formed the Societas Lutudarum (Lutudarum Company). Several stamped pigs of lead have been found which carry the name of the company with the cast inscription 'OCIORVM LVTVD BRIT. EX. ARG.' 'LVTVD' can be expanded to Latudarum, and 'EX ARG' to Ex Argentum which means silver free, so the inscription can be translated as 'The Latudarum Company, British silver-free lead.'

The Roman occupation of the Peak District played an important role in the development of the region and has left us with a number of cases of paranormal activity. It's not just the sound of the tramping feet of those legionnaires that is heard. Roman soldiers have actually been seen tramping across the ridge between Glossop and Hope.

In 1932, four climbers told how they and a terrified Alsatian dog had lain on the heather near Hope Cross and watched a Roman legion pass on the lane. Their description of the long, curved shields and the curious helmets of the warriors in full uniform, carrying standards was very convincing.

Other reports seem to emanate from the same area of the moors around Hope Cross and Wooller Knoll which lie directly on the route of the Roman road between Win Hill, Kinder Scout and Doctor's Gate. The sheer terror of the people who claim to have seen them is very genuine and according to park rangers who patrol that area, on at least two occasions, the people involved had to be taken to hospital.

Misty Shapes

We all rely upon our senses to interpret everyday happening whether they are sounds or sights, but all manner of things can be moulded by the human mind, bending reality to fit human expectation and legend.

It's not only sounds that baffle us, the swirling mists that so regularly shade the lonely highland peaks shroud trees that assume fantastic shapes, and add to its eerie nature. When a low bank of cloud covers the moors, it is not unusual for people to report seeing a threatening shape that is quite capable of reducing the observer to blind panic. Some people would argue that it's all in the mind of the witness – some sort of hallucination, or that the mind is simply re-running a familiar memory from inside the person's head, a sort of mental mirage.

If evidence of a psychic phenomena is based on only one person's account, there might be grounds for such sceptical suspicion, but when two or more people witness the same manifestation and others have reported the same thing over a period of years, this theory fails miserably.

The lonely landscape of the dark Peak where the hazy horizon seems to stretch into eternity.

However, in the case of the Roman legionnaires and many of the other phenomena reported here, these are not misty shapes. Numerous people have reported seeing the same thing, their descriptions and testimonies agree in every detail, so this can't be dismissed as an overactive imagination or a mental mirage.

The Phantom Planes of the Peak

It was 18 May 1945, just ten days after the Second World War had ended in Europe and the men of the Royal Canadian Air Force were just counting the days to 20 June when they were due to fly back home. A big send off was planned by the local people and their British colleagues but counting the days was a boring occupation for men used to action. To keep the men occupied, cross-country flights and routine exercises were undertaken by all the crews and on this day, the six-man crew of Lancaster KB993, part of the Royal Canadian Air Force 'Goose' Squadron, took off from RAF Linton-on-Ouse, for what was to be their final flight.

There are numerous sightings of ghostly grey aircraft flying over the Peak.

This experienced crew consisted of Flying Officer Anthony Arthur Clifford, Bomb Aimer 'Scratch' Fehrman, Wireless Operator 'Blood and Guts' Cameron, Air Gunners 'Hairless Joe' Halvorson and 'Rabbit' Hellerson, and Flight Engineer 'Gassless' McIver. They had been formed in 1941, just one of many RCAF squadrons which served at Allied bases overseas. Ironically on this fateful voyage, their navigator 'Gee Sam' had not accompanied them as they had only been cleared for local flying. They were taking a circular tour of the region, passing over South Yorkshire towards the Derbyshire border and the Peak District. Amidst the mist-shrouded Pennines, the plane suddenly plunged straight into James Thorn (map reference 077949) at full speed and burst into a ball of flame. Five of the crew died instantly, the rear gunner managed to crawl clear of the wreckage but died of his burns. Six men who had braved the war over Germany had been tragically killed in routine training, but this tragedy seemed to mark the beginning of a rather disturbing trend. Just two months later and 50yds away from the same site, a USAF Dakota crashed in similar circumstances killing its seven-man crew, and the tragic history continues with fifty planes in as many years coming down over this stretch of the Peak District moors.

But it is not just the mystery of the multiple crashes that perplex local people. Clairvoyants and psychics have been contacted by dead airmen, and a local farmer who rescued some of the wreckage to use as spare parts watched the barn where it

A Lancaster bomber flying over the Derwent Dam is making a return visit, but many people report seeing phantom planes too.

The ghostly figures of airmen have been seen beside the wreckage of their crashed planes and in the Hikers Bar of the Old Nags Head, which served as a temporary morgue.

was stored shake uncontrollably. He returned it to the crash site next day and things returned to normal.

There have been numerous sightings of ghostly grey aeroplanes which have been seen flying in eerie silence in action replays. Some people have even reported seeing the planes flying low before plunging down into the peaty bogs of the moorland to disappear without trace. Initially it was believed that the people who witnessed these paranormal flights were just recalling something they had previously viewed, until it was realised that most of the people who reported these replays of phantom planes have never seen them in reality. Other theories have been considered and found lacking too.

The ghostly figures of the men that perished have also been seen by hikers, campers and motorists. Phantom figures wearing flying jackets have been spotted hovering near their shattered flight decks. In fact sightings of ghostly planes and phantom airmen are so numerous that they have become woven into the rich tapestry of paranormal events that are rife in the area.

In April 1994, retired postman Tony Ingle was walking his dog Ben near the hill which overlooks the crash site of the Lancaster and Dakota when suddenly the sunshine overhead was blocked out by a propeller-driven plane which Tony later identified as a Dakota. He said he could see the propellers going round yet there was no sound, just a deadly silence. He watched the plane banking as it tried to turn, then it disappeared over the crest of the hill. Tony and Ben sprinted to the top of the hill and gazed down, convinced that the plane had come down, but the field was empty. Tony, who until then was a firm disbeliever in such things as ghosts, has regularly returned to the site to try to fathom just how such a thing could have happened, but Ben refuses to go anywhere near it. On one occasion when Tony tried to force him, Ben slipped his collar and ran.

For a long time, people have been seeing mystery aircraft plunging down on these moors and there have been fruitless searches for them. Sometimes there are numerous witnesses whose testimonies tally. Some of these witnesses are no-nonsense farmers who pooh-pooh the very idea of ghost stories yet admit that the Peakland hills have a means of tapping into some kind of memory field.

The Olde Nag's Head at Edale is the official starting point of the 270-mile Pennine Way and, as might be expected from a pub that dates back to 1577, there is a lot of spirit activity. The Hikers' Bar served as a temporary morgue during the war and following many plane crashes in the area, so this is where the bodies of the crashed airmen were brought and where their spirits still remain.

The Ghosts of Edale

Edale has a few ghostly tales of its own. The sound of galloping horses are regularly heard, and the most told story concerns three parish councillors who were returning from a meeting one evening. They heard the sound so distinctly that they thought they were runaways and the men took a stand in the road in order to stop them. There they stood waiting, but despite peering into the gloom they were unable to see the oncoming horses and stood helpless and amazed as the sound of beating hooves galloped past then died away in the distance.

More distressing is the prolonged, blood-curdling scream followed by a splash like a heavy weight or a body being pitched into the pool where the pack-horse bridge spans the tiny River Noe. These are the sounds that have been heard by many villagers and visitors, and are said to be the echo of an incident when a boy was dragged from the now ruined Edale Head Farm and drowned in the stream.

South Head Farm between Edale and Hayfield was a mid-seventeenth-century farm house that has now been demolished, but about three centuries ago, a murder was committed there. A jealous lover suspected the daughter of the house of being unfaithful and murdered her in her bedroom. After committing the foul deed, the murderer dragged the girl's body downstairs and across a field to dispose of it in a stream where he hoped it would be assumed she had died by accident or suicide. There was no record as to whether he got away with it or not, but mysteries have a way of leaking out.

The last tenants to occupy the farm were the Bradbury family, who often heard muffled bumps on the stairs and caught fleeting glimpses of a young woman in white in the fields between the farm and the stream. They began to suspect that they had a ghost; this was confirmed during the hay harvest when three Irish men were working as casual labourers on the farm. They knew nothing of the incident or the alleged ghost. Along with the farmer and his sons, they were making hay in the field between the farm and the stream when suddenly one of them enquired who the girl in white was running down to the stream. The Bradburys were surprised by the question as no one else could see the girl, but the Irish man was adamant he had seen a young woman running towards the stream where she promptly disappeared from sight.

Action Replays and the Electrical Impulse Wave Theory

Most apparitions are a complete repeat of an actual event that occurred many years earlier. It's a case of people returning and doing what they did in life. But how can inanimate objects somehow leave an impression of a long-ago event imprinted like a time recording? How can energy signals from emotive events become recorded in the ether? How can a whole scene turn into an action replay?

A catalogue of events tied to the trauma just before death, particularly if it is sudden or violent, seems able to imprint itself indelibly across time. When dealing with powerfully emotive events like ancient battles or plane crashes this emotional suffering could send out some kind of psychic distress flare that permanently alters the feeling or vibes of a place. In those situations, brain waves which can be recorded on an electro-encephalograph, become more active, and when they reach a certain pitch, it's possible that they can be picked up and stored by certain substances.

But action replay events are not always dramatic battles or murders, they can be amazingly trivial, a look back at what someone once did. A person who is sensitive to atmosphere may see, hear or sense the mood of a misty figure acting out what they did in life without any form of interaction with the 'viewer.'

Stone houses made of the local millstone which is rich in quartz crystals have more paranormal 'visitations' than brick houses. Quartz crystals vibrate when under pressure and generate a small charge of electrical energy, like in a watch, which can cause a chain reaction and allow us to tune into some form of time travel.

No one has yet found a fool-proof answer to how or why we are able to tap into this power, we just have to accept that something in the ether appears able to 'record' these things like a loop of film or a sound tape which can be rewound and played again for new audiences. It can happen at random times and in chance places so perhaps one day you might just be able to press that re-play button!

Ghost Lights

Over the centuries there have been continuous reports of strange lights in and around the Peak District. They form part of the local folklore. A strange glow above a hill in 1600 would be considered a ghost light of demonic origin, in 2000 it would be reported as a UFO, so explanations have changed but the lights remain.

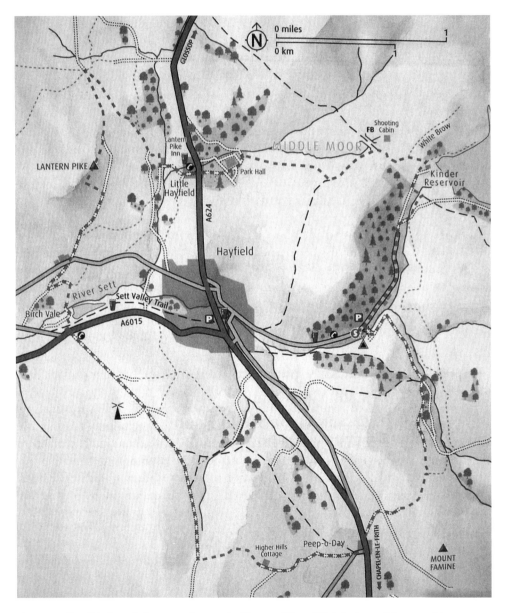

A strange yellow light is regularly seen on the summit of Lantern Pike, which is in the top-left corner of the map.

These ghost lights have a variety of names locally. There's Will-o-the-Wisp, Jack-Lantern, St Elmo's Fire or *Ignis Fatuus* from Medieval Latin, literally meaning foolish fire. Some regional lights are seen so regularly that they have been given individual names like Peggy wi' th' Lantern, which is a strange yellow light which entices foolish followers to their deaths high on the summit of Lantern Pike.

Our ancestors believed that mischievous fairies or evil spirits used lights to lead mesmerised travellers from their safe paths to bogs, mires and pools where they would be swallowed up. It's the stuff of fairytales, but what better theories do we have? The rapid playful movement of the lights suggested that they possessed some kind of low order of intelligence like luminous insects or elementals. In some areas, they were known as Spunkies, a dialect word for spark and were thought to be the souls of unbaptized children doomed to wander the earth till Judgement Day. They move up and down in crazy patterns far too quickly for them to be the lights of a car or motorbike and some people believe they even relate to people.

Over marshland these sightings are readily explained as marsh gases. The rotting vegetation and animal matter produces a chemical soup that bubbles up through the bog letting off unctuous, condensed vapours. When ignited this could produce wispy flames, but what ignites these gases? Also the vapours would be more likely to burn on the surface rather than float upwards and hover as if caught and carried by air currents.

Ghostly lights are often seen on mountains and rocky gritstone uplands. They appear around outcrops like Lunter Rocks above the village of Winster and Harborough Rocks near Brassington. They hover over old standing stones like Arbor Low and Stanton Moor and although these strange elusive lights seem to prefer the gritstone areas of the northern Peak District, there have also been reports around Dovedale and the Manifold Valley.

One explanation is that the local millstone rocks are rich in quartz crystals which vibrate when under pressure, so these earthlights could be the natural light emissions squeezed out of the rocks under geographical stress to create an atmospheric glow. Quartz crystals are used in watches and cigarette lighters where the pressure button crushes a crystal, causing a vibration and generating a tiny surge of electrical energy which provides the spark that can ignite flammable gases. Could a mass of quartz-bearing rock produce an electrical signal that causes a chain reaction and triggers glowing spook lights that can be seen in the surrounding atmosphere?

The parish records at Chapel en le Frith dated 30 March 1716 seem to have recorded Derbyshire's oldest reported incident of strange, bright lights which were seen in the sky between the hours of 9 p.m. and midnight. Apparently it was bright enough to read a book by. Nearly 300 years later, people are still reporting them to the mountain rescue team, in the belief that they are distress flares.

The Longdendale Lights which haunt the gritstone crags on the north face of Bleaklow have been reported for so long they have become part of the folklore of the region. Sometimes called the Devil's Bonfires, they are also linked to the phantom legions of Roman soldiers who tramp across the darkened moors on the first night of

Above and below: *Ghostly lights are a regular feature of Peakland folklore.*

the first full moon in the spring. The ghostly glow is said to be flames from the torches carried by the auxiliaries marching along the route of a Roman road linking the fort at Glossop with the Hope Valley. The string of moving lights have been mistaken for hiker's torches high on the mountainside, searchlight beams, distress flares, ball lighting, or rare electrical phenomena. Walkers who become disorientated as darkness falls have seen the lights and, believing them to be a distant village, have followed them only to find the lights continued to move away from them.

On 28 January 1989, the Charlesworth family of New Mills reported a midnight sighting that lasted about three minutes. Three of them watched and debated. They described it as unmoving and lighting up the valley like a floodlight. It had rays of light coming out, and then all of a sudden it was not there any more. At first they thought it might be a car headlight but when they later compared this with a car on the hillside it was nothing like it. The alien light was much brighter, and about half the size of the full moon.

On 22 February 1993 four people were driving near Devil's Elbow around 8.40 p.m. They all reported seeing a strange white glow in the north-east towards Mossley. There is a pulsing light in the area, the beacon of the Holme Moss television transmitter mast. When seen through mist this can be quite eerie, but in most instances this is ruled out completely.

Not all reports are of night sightings. On 20 December 1988 at 7.40 a.m. a man was riding his moped from Ellaston to work at Ashbourne when he spotted a pyramid of light in the sky. He experienced a peculiar sense of calm, then suddenly the pyramid of light had gone but the man was feeling unwell and his motorbike was malfunctioning. His pounding headache, sore eyes, dizziness and tingling sensation like pins and needles (all classic witness symptoms widely reported after experiencing such energy encounters) gradually subsided, but what he couldn't explain was the time-lapse. He had lost a considerable number of minutes.

On 27 August 1984 two science technicians from Sheffield were hiking around Edale when they saw a spherical shining ball moving down the hill. They were able to watch it for several minutes and discuss what it might be. It was only a few inches in diameter, but clearly self-propelled and floating – yet also controlled. It rose over a group of trees, hovered, followed the course of the Hope to Edale road, and then climbed at speed until it disappeared in the clouds. Checks later revealed that it could not have been a toy balloon as it was moving against the wind.

In April 1983, two doctors on a walking holiday spotted a silver-blue ball. It was 1 p.m. on a perfectly clear day – allowing them to witness the object as it drifted across Sykes Moor before rising suddenly and rapidly into the clouds.

Similar reports abound in the Peak District, but we are no nearer reaching a satisfactory answer as to what these lights are. How can they be marsh gases out in space, way above the nearest horizontal surface? Some form of glowing nocturnal insect like a firefly is ruled out because even if they were really much closer than they seemed, the reported light anomalies are far too big for fireflies. And they are still being experienced.

In 2007, the strange blue and green lights that appeared above Matlock during a heavy snow storm are still something of a meteorological mystery. The phenomenon which also caused house lights to flicker was seen at around 7.15 p.m. and witness Rob Brook of Tansley said it was accompanied by a sound like something out of *Close Encounters*. A spokesman for the Met Office initially suggested it could have been lightning refracted through the snow, but following more detailed analysis, a report prepared by the Met Office for the *Matlock Mercury* said:

> A quick look at the lightning location data on 9 February in the Matlock area, shows that our system detected no lightning at the times of interest, or indeed outside of these times. The system has a variable detection efficiency and does not guarantee to sense all lightning activity that occurs. It is also optimised to detect cloud to ground lightning, which is usually the more powerful lightning, rather than inter or intra cloud lightning. However, what was seen in this snow event may have more to do with electrostatic charging in the snow. Sandstorms and blizzards are known to cause such charging.

If you have any alternative theory then email news@matlockmercury.co.uk.

Change Causes Paranormal Activity

Many supernatural phenomena are stimulated by change. Ask any home owner who has revamped an old house. They disturb a lot of spirit activity. My theory is that spirits get used to the electrical energy that is around the people that inhabit their building. When those people move out, the energy changes and they are confused and disorientated. They show their uncertainty by opening and closing doors, moving things, and turning music on and off. Once the new owners have settled in and the energy levels are stable again, the spirits can settle again.

It's rather the same in the environment where earth energies are stored in the ground. Areas will remain generally quiet as a picturesque part of the landscape, then every now and then something upsets the delicate balance of forces and a frantic period of activity erupts. Any major disturbances, whether natural or man-made, will cause these earth energies to leak out, so there is likely to be activity around quarries and reservoirs where fault lines and earth tremors occur.

In the past when a new well was dug, a road made or the railway was being constructed these earthworks seemed to disturb the balance and activate something odd. When the London & North Western Railway was constructing their line north, they found that foundations sank, bridge sections collapsed and workmen fell ill. Locals whispered about the consequence that could be expected if the Ward was upset. Eventually, the railway company and contractors gave up battling with the malign power and sited an alternative route (*see* 'Dicky's Skull – the Cranial Guardian of Tunstead Farm' in Chapter 4).

Mystery and Mayhem on the Motorway

The M1 motorway which gives millions of people access to the Peak District was started on 23 August 1965, but encountered problems right from the beginning. Bad weather conditions, an investigation of some 800 magnetic anomalies in the soil formation, and major subsidence associated with an area riddled with uncharted mine shafts was just the start. Within a decade of its opening, there had been many horrendous accidents and they have continued regularly since. Although some problems may be exacerbated by the design of the road, people regularly report strange phenomena that can't be dismissed as hallucinations, and the motorway has became directly associated in the popular imagination with hauntings.

In March 1978, the *Derbyshire Times* ran the story that a stretch of the M1 at Pinxton near junction 28 has more than its fair share of accidents. This section is often fog-bound when no other is, claimed the paper, but is this a natural fog? Suggestions have been made that the motorway crosses the direct path where a ghost is alleged to walk, although as yet, this ghostly entity has not been identified.

The Notorious Stocksbridge Bypass

It is possible that the notoriously dangerous Stocksbridge bypass could blame its paranormal activity on the fact that it was opened on Friday 13th – 13 May 1988 to be precise – yet the problems began long before then. The ghostly phenomena started even before work began in the autumn of 1987, on the £14 million bypass. There were claims that the construction work had disturbed a graveyard, and as the builders sliced through earth and crags, stories from local folklore began to surface. It was claimed that a ghostly stage-coach is seen charging along the rutted tracks. The area also claimed to be haunted by the spirits of children killed in mining accidents, and a holy man who was not buried in consecrated ground is said to roam the area.

It is therefore not surprising that this seven-mile highway which links the M1 with the A616 Manchester road has developed a reputation for being jinxed. In fact, there are so many reports of a paranormal nature that the full story is featured in our chapter entitled 'Road and Rail Frights'.

Quarries Kick-Start Earth Energies into Life

Quarries abound within the Pennines and there is a close correlation between them and the lights, humming noises and other paranormal phenomena reported in the area. Mining and blasting work disturbs the ground in the same way that building a road or sinking a well does, releasing the wrath of the spirits and kick-starting earth energy into life.

Quarries like this one in the Peak District kick-start earth energy into life.

The Standbark Boggart Stops Matlock Development

For over ten years, residents of Matlock have been watching progress on a housing development at a disused quarry to the east of the main Matlock to Darley Dale road. This 130-acre site on three distinct levels would provide much-needed housing in a desirable residential area, yet right from the start the operation has been jinxed.

Owned and worked by Tarmac Co. Ltd, when production ceased they tried for many years to get planning permission for housing and industry without success. The immense cost of installing the necessary relief road made it unviable for them and in 1994 it was sold to A.P.H. Properties. To pay for the development it was decided to offer the lower plateau to a supermarket, one of the upmarket ones preferably, because Matlock and district was considered A1 housing.

Two public meetings were held and members of the public were asked to air their views. Some did it in writing and the most unexpected letter of protest, although unsigned, came from someone who stated that the development would never go ahead because the Standbark Boggart would not allow it. Bearing in mind that this multi-million-pound development scheme was the biggest ever considered in the area, the councillors of the Derbyshire Dales District were treading very carefully, but even so, such a letter was dismissed as superstitious mumbo jumbo. Planning Officer Roger Yarwood made the comment, 'I think we would have trouble sustaining a planning appeal on the basis of disturbing a ghost.'

The civic society was very much in favour of the scheme, but the local traders objected saying it would affect their trade. People were unsure what was happening and many rumours circulated, so in 1998 when Sainsbury's bought ten acres of the site and put in a planning application for a supermarket and car park, they had a scale model built and put it on public display. The Summerfield store in the town put up a lot of opposition which delayed matters for two years.

To gain access to the site a new road had to be constructed. To do this it was necessary to remove the arcade and the weeping beech tree in front of the Bank of Scotland. The semi-circular arcade was examined and found to be made of reconstituted stone dating only from the 1950s and would be easy to re-site or replace. A prominent botanist was brought in to examine the tree and he pointed out the dead wood inside the spread and expressed an opinion that it would be dead in twenty years anyway due

5 respondents expressed concern about the loss of the weeping beech and colonnade in front of the Royal Bank of Scotland but these letters were written before the proposals were changed to offer protection to these features. 3 respondents refer to the desirability of safeguarding trees generally within the Cawdor Quarry area.

4 respondents ask the District Council to have regard to the wildlife and ecological value of certain parts of the quarry and/or the site of Special Scientific Importance.

3 respondents ask for care to be shown in the selection of materials and the design of the development.

3 respondents refer to the necessity to improve public transport provision and 2 refer to the need for good pedestrian links between the supermarket and the Town Centre.

3 respondents refer to difficulties which may be encountered relating to the geological situation within the quarry, the existence of lead mines and/or the presence of toxic waste.

Other relevant issues which are raised but do not occur in more than two letters are:-

- the need to exploit the river frontage;
- concern about the proximity of the industrial development to housing;
- the future use of Halldale and its affect on the development.

Lastly, one respondent expresses concern about the effect of the scheme on the "Standbark Boggart", who apparently roams this territory. The respondent refers to dire consequences which may follow from disturbing this ghost!

The planning meeting document listing respondent's queries concerning the planned development of Cawdor Quarry, Matlock, and the first mention of the Standbark Boggart.

Commercial buildings on the Cawdor Quarry site were affected by strange goings-on.

to the carbon-monoxide poisoning caused by the queuing traffic in the area. The Bank of Scotland was extremely accommodating about the whole thing, but 'Joe Public' were up in arms about it. Bowing to public pressure the only alternative was to apply for special permission to make a slight deviation in the road, something that is not allowed on any new major road. This wasted two years.

Suggestions to bypass the 100-year-old bridge which is a listed ancient monument met more opposition. British Rail wanted £1,500,000 to move a length of track 50yds for better alignment. Matlock Angling Club protested about losing their fishing rights on the river because of the new bridge that would span it and naturalists objected too because of the fossils in the rock faces, and the site was given an Sight of Special Scientific Interest (SSSI) status. New flooding regulations meant that a large stretch of Bakewell Road had to be raised 2m. All the delays and hidden costs meant that the price of developing the site was escalating out of control.

A small amount of industry still continued, but as the buildings became vacant, they were getting vandalised. The site was open to fly-tipping and New Age travellers moved in. It became known in the underworld as a spot for 'raves'. Drugs were rife and at one rave a boy climbed up on a 40ft-high roof and fell through. He had to be airlifted to hospital.

The whole operation met with problems at every stage, but you remember that initial letter about the Standbark Boggart! Was he actually responsible? Strange things had begun happening at Cawdor Commercials who manufactured truck bodies in one of the large buildings on the site. These men were tough no-nonsense guys who didn't believe in ghosts, or at least they hadn't until things got so bad they could find no other explanation. In the office corridor, people have heard sounds which correspond exactly with the measured tread of human footsteps. They stop as they reach the door. No one ever appears, and the corridor was always empty. Cold draughts were often felt in the corridor and one member of the office staff was trapped in the toilet by an unseen, though felt, presence. Another regular sound was the banging on the sides of the building, which was made of corrugated sheeting. Again, when going to check, no one was ever there and it was impossible for any troublesome person playing a prank to have got away without being seen.

There was always the sense of being watched, and followed. People were touched, machinery malfunctioned and the overhead crane mysteriously moved. The forks of the fork-lift truck fell down nearly scaring the workers to death. For safety reasons, it was never left with the forks in the air. As one of the men said:

> It wasn't just the fact that no one was near it, or the fact that the forks should not have been up, it was the way it fell as if someone was watching our reaction and deliberately paused it mid-fall to get the maximum response. It was lever operated and just too spooky for it to be an accidental fall.

Prior to this the company operated a night shift, but from then on the guys were too scared and all refused to work at night. It wasn't long after this that they re-sited the company away from the area.

The Cawdor Quarry development was a stop-and-start operation right from the very start. In 1998, Chelvaton Land Development Co. bought it out. They went bankrupt and sold to Groveholt in 2001. Groveholt got permission for 480 houses and in the meantime, the cost of development had shot up from £3,700,000 in 1996 to £10,000,000 in 2004

In 2006 it looked as though all the problems had eventually been ironed out when new legislation was introduced stating that after a number of horrendous accidents on railways, any road that ran alongside a railway line had to have 8ft concrete barriers running alongside. This would have meant that an unsightly barrier ran the whole length of the site, so a complete new site layout had to be devised with the road running through the estate rather than around it. The Environment Agency in the meantime had decided that much of the land was below the new flood level and must be built up and so the delays continue. At the time of writing, the new site plan is awaiting approval, but the current recession is now taking its toll with no building work scheduled for the foreseeable future.

If the Standbark Boggart is responsible for all this confusion and chaos he's certainly a powerful force to reckon with and, if and when the housing does materialise, what vengeance is he likely to heap on those unsuspecting householders?

two

IDOLS, HEATHEN GODS AND NATURE SPIRITS

The Power of the Stones

The Peak District is fortunate to have reminders of our Celtic ancestors littered across a number of chambered tombs, stone circles and burial mounds sited on prominent hills. Some were given the name 'low' from the Old English word *hlaw* meaning hill.

The study of these places is called stone lore, and it is said that the stones at such sites have much in common. This list is not complete and in no particular order of importance, but just goes to show what you might expect. They are said to: have healing powers, aid conception, attract lightning if interfered with, hold electrical

Tentatively testing the power of the stones.

energy, be unable to be counted, be capable of a rocking or turning movement (when no one is looking), and to have once been people turned into stone for transgressing a local taboo.

Some people who touch the stones are able to feel the energy and there are even claims that it is possible to get a mild electric shock. Others touch the stones while holding a crystal on a length of chain and find that the crystal moves of its own accord. I used divining rods to sense these unusual energies and I was not disappointed. People who are particularly sensitive to changes in atmospheric pressure report hearing faint sounds like whining, humming or buzzing much like those emitted from transformers and power lines.

Many people have experienced a sense of languor at these ancient sites and it has been suggested that heightened natural radiation can perhaps engender this feeling. If this is so, it is possible that this factor was used by our ancestors to help promote ritual sleep at such sites. Certain geophysical conditions might also affect the subconscious mind, which may account for some of the previous claims, and, although you might think this is purely local folklore, these facts are recognised at similar ancient sites throughout the world.

Earth Energy at Sacred Sites

In June 1921 Alfred Watkins rediscovered ley lines. Many people said he actually discovered them, but that is not so: they are the remains of old trading tracks laid down in Britain in the Neolithic period of roughly 5000–2000 BC. Watkins recognised the fact that the leys, which we tend to call ley lines, had been initially sited from one hilltop to the next in alignment, and the hilltops were marked with standing stones, cairns and earth mounds, each visible from the next. In many cases, the leys ran across the countryside linking ancient Celtic or Druidic points of worship. With fallen stones and modern obstructions this line is now impaired but I was fascinated to find that in Derbyshire, Arbor Low, Stanton Moor and Ashover Fabric all sit on the same line of latitude and a very obvious ley line.

Leys are well submerged both actually, beneath accretions of buildings and earth, and metaphorically, beneath layers of time, so what made Watkin's findings so fascinating was his pronouncement that these leys were in fact energy channels, and where they cross, powerful forces are concentrated. With this discovery came the realisation that ancient man didn't just erect monuments on any old hill, he knew how to tap, augment and utilise these earth energies.

The tribal shaman experienced visions and used intuition rather like the mediums and psychics of today, so if a shaman recognized some location as special, a place where the energy was at its strongest, the whole tribe would take note and the ancient markers such as stone circles and megaliths would be focused there. These stone circles functioned as communal temples and meeting places so that as they worshipped, the people could benefit from the earth's power.

Above and below: *Arbor Low is a mystical place; the stones now lie flat but do they still possess magical powers?*

The idea that some invisible force spider-webbed the British landscape with lines like some Neolithic energy grid understandably caused quite a controversy and all kinds of new theories began to surface. It was claimed that these unusual energies leak from the earth at suitable release points to be seen like a transparent heat haze that sprays into the air before dispersing and disappearing. At its most powerful, this energy leaks out into the atmosphere creating visual changes in the air which creates radio and television interference, power overloads, and temporary disruptions to street lighting. Sometimes this causes particles to be charged and transformed into glowing effects in the atmosphere rather like disco lights.

Ancient man would have been aware of these bursts of energy activity and the sounds that are often heard at sites renowned as holy and special. Derbyshire's Arbor Low and the Nine Ladies stone circle remain sanctified pagan sites while other sites were later Christianised by having a church or cross superimposed on them, and the leys were often referred to as holy lines or archaic tracks.

Arbor Low

The great henge and stone circle at Arbor Low near Monyash are some of the finest examples left by early man, and have become known as the Stonehenge of Derbyshire. For many hundreds of years, people would have travelled here from miles around to worship their gods and ask for help with the harvest or to ensure the continued fertility of the land and community.

Arbor Low is on the summit of a hill 375m above sea level. Although it is a bleak, windy place, the view on a fine day is stunning. The low comprises a circular bank 76m in diameter by 2m high with entrances at the north-west and south-east. Inside is a ditch about 1.5m deep enclosing a circular central sanctuary area where there are roughly fifty-nine different sized stones all now lying flat. No one knows if the stones once stood upright but it could be that the early Christians decided they smacked too much of their pagan origins and laid them down in order to 'de-sanctify' the site.

A core element of many ancient, sacred henges and monuments was the astronomical aspects that were built into their structure. These orientations linked them with the heavens and surrounding landscape so that the midwinter sun would shine directly down the entrance passage or along the main axis, or some central gap framed the midsummer sunrise or other significant lunar event. This association with ancient astronomy is one of the reasons why traditional festivals that reach back to pagan origins still take place there. Such festivals relate to the astronomical divisions of the solar year – the solstices, equinoxes and the 'cross quarter' days between. These are Imbolc (February), Beltane (May), Lughnassadh (August) and Samhain (November).

Arbor Low is a mystical place where many spirits are said to dwell. Remember the belief that the old stones can promote fertility? Given the cold and windy location, those involved in the act of procreation would need superhuman powers or an implausibly strong belief in the power of the stones.

Rowter Rocks and the Druid Inn, Birchover

Next to the Druid Inn at Birchover stands an impressive pile of gritstone megaliths known as Rowter Rocks. These heaps of rocks form majestic mounds piled high, smoothed and weathered into abstract shapes that are immensely impressive. It helps to be as nimble as a mountain goat to climb up, through and round them, and beware of the steep drop disguised by the overgrown vegetation, and the chasms that seem to be bottomless. There are alcoves and caves that reach deep into the inner core, so it is advisable to take a torch to explore these.

Right and overleaf: *Rowter Rocks are said to be haunted by malevolent spirits.*

Over to one side are a series of hewn steps that lead to a reasonably flat stone mass. What singles this out for special attention is that at some time, it would appear to have had an elongated notch hewn to form seating complete with back support. But what makes this different is the two armrests that divide the seat into three, rather like seats in a cinema. As the name of the inn would imply, this area has the reputation of being a former stronghold of Druid worship and the area is rich with evidence of primitive man's passage. So is it fanciful to speculate that this was the seat of the Arch-Druid? Ranked by his advisers, he could have sat and surveyed the landscape stretched out in front of him, because Rowter Rocks command the most amazing views. Sitting here surveying the scene, it is not difficult to see why an ancient site like this has long been regarded as a place of power where unusual forces can manifest. Folk memory, rumours and anecdotes from visitors have been augmented by the claims of psychics, so there is a wealth of evocative tales associated with Rowter Rocks.

The Druid Inn is haunted by an old lady who made her presence known.

Some say the place is haunted by many malevolent spirits. A cloaked, ghostly figure is the most frequently seen, although on moonlit nights it is said that the whole area is filled with the sound of weeping and wailing. Local legend says that if you sit in the afore-mentioned middle armchair when the church clock has just struck midnight, you will hear the spirit of the wind whisper the name of your true love. Personally, due to the hazardous drops this is one place I'd never venture at night without a couple of arc lights and an ambulance standing by.

A visit to the Druid Inn is a must for anyone visiting Rowter Rocks. After partaking of the hospitality of the house, I questioned the friendly staff to learn more about the paranormal activity of the area and especially about the a kindly old lady with the warm, caring smile who is alleged to sit in the corner of one of the downstairs rooms. My enquiries seemed to be going nowhere when suddenly a magazine that had been on a unit in the corner of the room suddenly fell on the floor. I recognised the magazine as one which I occasionally write for, and as I took it from the waiter, it fell open at one of my articles. Was this just a coincidence? Perhaps, but what are the odds against that kind of thing happening?

Stanton Moor

In the eighteenth century, it was the custom of large landowners to entertain their guests by taking them on a tour of their estates in horse-drawn carriages. The scenic drive or ride along the edge of Stanton Moor formed the boundary between the Stanton estate and the Haddon estate. It is still known as the Duke's Drive and with its panoramic views would have been a popular drive for the Duke of Rutland's London guests.

The Duke's Drive is only one track. Across the moor are numerous other hollowed-out pathways in the heather that would have been eroded by the hooves of the lines of thirty or forty packhorses. These have now become the walks and recreational routes used by today's visitors who walk across the moor, to discover an area which is rich in stone circles, burial mounds and other remnants of our ancient past. It is also rich in stories that include abduction by UFOs, reports of a spectral black dog, a ghostly monk, a headless horseman, a green man, a white lady and hovering lights. All these stories add to the atmosphere of the place, but most people associate Stanton Moor with the Nine Ladies stone circle.

Modern-day witches with their respect for nature still meet on Stanton Moor and report a strong energy force in the area of the Nine Ladies circle, which is 35ft in diameter and surrounded by a shallow mound. To the south-west of the circle is the King Stone or as some call it, the Fiddler's Chair. According to legend, the Devil played his fiddle while nine ladies danced on the Sabbath, but God was so furious at their transgression that he turned them all into stone for disregarding his holy day. It's a story that is attached to many similar stone circles, but instead of being called ladies, they are called 'maidens' which is believed to be a corruption of 'meyn' meaning stone. This may be inchoate folk memory and over time was changed to ladies.

Stanton Moor is a bleak moorland plateau dotted with stones and burial mounds.

Whatever, there they still remain in their petrified state on this lonely moor, and when the wind blows across the hillside you can almost hear the screeching sound of a fiddle being played badly. A ghostly male figure dressed in black has often been seen standing just outside the circle. Could this be the Devil or the fiddler, or just a trick of the light?

The Nine Ladies circle on Stanton Moor. The stones are, according to legend, nine ladies that danced on the Sabbath. They were turned to sone for their transgression.

Remarkable Stones

It takes thousands of years of sand-laden wind to slowly sculpt the rock masses that litter the Peak District, but if you look on an ordnance survey map you'll find that specific rock formations have been given fanciful names like the Cakes of Bread, Two Penny Loaf Rock, Eagle Stone, Cork Stone, Toad's Mouth Rock and so on. It takes a little imagination to see the rock's resemblance to its name up close, but most have a striking appearance from a distance. Some say that Ashover Fabric which stands majestically 980ft above the Derbyshire village was once the site of a Druid temple; some believe it's the centre of a number of converging ley lines, but most people simply enjoy its panoramic views encompassing Derbyshire, Yorkshire, Lincolnshire, Nottinghamshire, Leicestershire and Staffordshire.

There also seems to be a predominance of Rocking or Turning Stones. Many of these stone have been dislodged or wedged for safety purposes and I was interested to read about one such stone at Chatsworth and the reason why it is now wedged. During the Second World War, 250 girls ranging in age from eleven to eighteen, and

Many impressive rock formations are given fanciful names.

thirty-six staff from Penrhos College, a girls boarding school situated on the sea front in Colwyn Bay, were evacuated to Chatsworth. Their stay began on 26 September 1939 and ended on 21 March 1946. They lived in Chatsworth House and played in the grounds and according to Nancie Park in her book *Personal Memoirs of the War Years at Chatsworth*, one of the popular attractions was the Moving Stone. This was a vast stone which when pushed, went round slowly like a revolving door in a hotel. One day in a rush of excitement and enthusiasm, Nancie apparently crushed her right leg in this. The bruising was impressive and she was in bed for a week and from then on the stone was wedged, making it non-movable. Apparently after all these years, her leg still has a weak spot on that knee.

Another turning stone is in an isolated outcrop of weathered gritstone, now almost submerged under a blanket of invasive rhododendron and accessed via a footpath to Cocking Tor off Holestone Gate Road, Ashover. It is impossible to turn the stone manually although it will rock to and fro upon its precarious pedestal by applying surprisingly little pressure. So why is it called a turning stone? Because legend says that the stone turns of its own accord when Ashover Church clock strikes midnight.

Some stones are capable of rocking or turning.

The Celts and the Little People

When the Romans invaded England, the surviving Celts headed for the hills and swamps where they could seemingly vanish without trace when pursued. Being small in stature, they became known as the little people. They possessed a wide knowledge of herbs and poisons which were unknown to the Romans, so stories grew up that the little people possessed magical powers. The poison arrows they used while out hunting were called fairy arrows and can be seen in museums today. This all added to the growing feeling that there really were supernatural creatures around, and this is where the image of the goblin, fairy, elf, kelpie and all the other magical beings that are reported widely in Peakland folklore took root.

The Magical Hob

Places where sightings of small, imp-like creatures were common have left us with names like Puxhill and Eldon, hill of the goblins and home of elves respectively. There's Hob Lane, Hob Tor and Hob Hurst from Old English *hyrst*, meaning hillock or copse, the home of the wood elf or hob. The hob was another form of elf or goblin and was sometimes called a hob-goblin. Hob was well known to our ancestors who would leave small quantities of food and drink in a special place to placate this spirit of nature because hobs were notorious for their mischievousness unless placated. Our ancestors believed that when hob was good he was magical, but when upset, he could cause havoc.

It's quite a trek over the rough, bracken-covered moorland to reach Hob Hurst's House which lies on the southern edge of Gibbet Moor and Bunker's Hill Wood, a deeply wooded hillside above Chatsworth. Hob Hurst's House is in fact a Bronze-Age burial mound, 32ft in diameter, and surrounded by a square ditch and bank. It is thought to date from 1600 to 1000 BC and is one of the least known prehistoric sites in Derbyshire. When a pile of scorched human bones were discovered at Hob Hurst's House in an archaeological dig carried out by Thomas Bateman in June 1853, the legend took on a macabre element, and the place now has a reputation for being the haunt of demonic forces.

The Power of the Little People

Our ancestors had great faith in the power of those small, often invisible creatures they called the little people. If the little people or fairy folk were particularly displeased with a human they would cast a curse. The person would become ill and could even die. The cows ran dry or the milk went sour. If they were so inclined or you happened to walk across some enchanted fairy ground known as the 'stray sod,' you lost your way. Many stories relate to travellers being led into the wild moorland and becoming helplessly lost because of the little people. Crossing a stray sod, you were likely to feel a

In exchange for a small quantity of food and drink, a hob would perform all kinds of useful tasks.

deathly cold blast known as a 'fairy wind' or a 'goath shee', which could leave a person paralysed.

Near Demons Dale in the parish of Taddington is a hill called Great Fin, noted for the very green spots that dot its slopes. To local villagers these were fairy rings, owing their greenness to the moonlight revels of the little people. Many sightings were alleged of fairies dressed in green, dancing hand in hand around their rings to the music of the field cricket, grasshopper or drone bee, aided in their joyous movements by the light of numerous glow-worms.

The presence of fungi and mushrooms is the real, if rather less exciting, cause of the greenness of fairy rings and in Derbyshire young mushrooms are often referred to as 'fairy buttons.' As they decay, local lore acknowledges that the Devil has been at work on them and driven out the fairies.

These romantic stories that conjure up pictures of mystical fairy folk dancing under the light of the moon have now been totally squashed by scientists who have proved that fairy rings are no more than the habit of some fungi to grow outwards from the centre, like the spokes of a wheel.

The Fairy Find

In 2007, I came across a story that was posted on a website by Dan Baines a local artist and magician. It read:

> While walking his dog along an old Roman road between Duffield and Belper, a local man who wishes to remain anonymous, made a very strange find – the mummified body of a fairy.
>
> The 8" remains complete with wings, skin, teeth and flowing red hair have been examined by anthropologists and forensic experts who can confirm that the body is genuine. X-rays of the fairy reveal an anatomically identical skeleton to that of a child. The bones however are hollow like those of a bird making them particularly light. The puzzling presence of a navel even suggests that the beings reproduce the same as humans despite the absence of reproductive organs.

According to Mr Baines, the response was phenomenal. The website quickly received thousands of visitors interested in the Derbyshire fairy and its author was inundated with emails on the subject. It was posted on other websites, forums and blogs, then on 1 April, Dan Baines added a statement to the website confessing that the fairy was a fake, an April Fool's Day prank. He wrote:

The 8in mummified body of a fairy, complete with wings, skin, teeth and flowing red hair.

Even if you believe in fairies as I personally do, there will always have been an element of doubt in your mind that would suggest that the remains are a hoax. However, the magic created by the possibility of the fairy being real is something you will remember for the rest of your life.

Alas the fairy is a fake but my interest and belief has allowed me to create a work of art that is convincing and magical. I was also interested to see if fairy folklore is still a valid belief in modern society and I am pleased to say that yes, it is. I have had more response from believers than I ever thought possible.

On 8 April 2007 the fairy was sold on eBay for £280 and, according to the BBC, is now in a private collection in the United States.

The Elementals

The elaborate fairy hoax just goes to prove that many people still believe that invisible nature spirits live in and rule over the four elements of the natural world: gnomes rule the earth, salamanders, the fire; sylphs, the air; and undines the water.

Earth spirits live deep within the earth in barrows, rocks, caves and quarries. Some, like the hobs and brownies, will attach themselves to certain families and prove useful in menial tasks, but some like the Boggart are vengeful spirits that cause problems.

The sylphs that live in the air are elusive spirits that have the ability to cause storms and heavy winds. Like some sort of luminous insect, the sylphs are often blamed for the rapid playful movement of the lights periodically seen throughout the Peak District.

Salamanders are considered temperamental. They are made up of fire, so if they became hostile, beware!

Undines or water nymphs are to be found in any body of water from oceans to wells. With their gossamer wings, it is said that their clothes change colour to blend with the water.

The Corn Dolly

Our pre-Christian ancestors endeavoured to please the spirits, so a series of animistic rituals grew up and some are still practiced today. One such survival is the corn dolly. It was believed that a nature spirit resided in each field of corn, so at harvest time, the last sheaf was cut with great care in order to preserve the spirit of the corn. This was then made into a corn dolly – the word 'dolly' is derived from the word idol. The spirit was preserved in the dolly during the winter, and then in the spring, the dolly was broken up and mixed with the seed corn in order to transfer the spirit back to the soil to ensure a good harvest.

A simple corn dolly holds the spirit of the corn.

The Spirit in the Stone

When lovers carve their initials within the shape of a heart on a tree trunk or rock, they are following an ancient custom, and knowingly or otherwise asking for the blessing of the nature spirits that reside within. The Wishing Stone located at Lumsdale near Matlock was enormously popular with the Victorians, who were great advocates of the power of nature spirits. They believed that if you walked round the stone three times while reciting your wish, it would be granted by the spirit or gnome that dwelt within.

The Wishing Stone at Lumsdale, Matlock.

Wishing Wells and Well Dressings

Few of us can resist the urge to throw a few coins in a wishing well, but how many of us realise we are actually following the ancient ritual of making an offering to the water spirit? It may not be a ceremonious ritual, but it's based on the same principle – we are asking the water spirit, in return for our offerings, to implement our wish.

We can trace this custom back to the Celtic tribes of the High Peak. They worshipped a water-goddess called Arnemetiae, 'the goddess beside the sacred grove,' who had an important shrine at Buxton's thermal spring. This was later developed by the Romans and became second only in importance to Bath which the Romans called Aquae Sulis. Buxton was named Aquae Arnemetiae

The custom of well-dressing almost certainly developed from the age-old fear and worship of water-gods and spirits, but a decree of AD 960 banned such practices and in 1102 St Anselm condemned well-dressing as idolatry. Water worship was strictly forbidden, but people still wanted to give thanks for the precious gift of water, so the practice was absorbed into Christianity with a few adaptations. At Buxton, the goddess Arnemetia became St Anne. It was a case of bending the rules slightly and re-dedicating the wells. It was then okay to dress the wells again provided it was for the Glory of God, but Derbyshire is perhaps the only place that has continued the beautiful old custom of well-dressing which still takes place today.

The folk tale of 'Hob o' the Hearth and the Old Woman' is a timeless treasure that generations of local children have grown up with. Hob moved into the cottage of a lonely old woman where he cleaned and cooked, then in the summer when Hob

An idol of the water goddess Arnemetiae. (Courtesy of Buxton Museum)

moved into the garden, the water in the well became sweeter to drink and softer to bathe in. The old woman's aches and pains became less and as a thank you to Hob, she decorated the well with beautiful flowers. The local villagers saw the beautiful well-flowers and decided to copy her example and so the custom of well-dressing began.

In reality, well-dressing in Tissington, where this tale originated, can be traced back to 1350. When neighbouring villages were hit with the deadly plague, Tissington alone remained immune and this was credited to the purity of their water.

A Victorian poster advertising the Well-Dressings. (Courtesy of Buxton Museum)

A dressed well at Tissington in 2008, where the origin of well-dressing can be traced back to 1350.

Crooker and the Traveller

It wasn't just the nature spirits in the wells, people regularly made offering to the nature spirits in the rivers in order to placate them and prevent them from taking lives. When travel was fraught with all kinds of dangers, travellers had good reason to give thanks for their safe passage and to pray for an uneventful conclusion to their journey. A bridge chapel like the one at Cromford beside the fifteenth-century bridge provided a sanctuary where travellers would give thanks for a safe journey completed or about to begin. Although the chapel is now a ruin it is one of only six that still survive in the whole country. Another is on the Derwent at Derby.

The fast-flowing River Derwent, or Darrant as it was known, was regarded almost as a deity who required respect and the occasional appeasement with human life. The stretch of river which runs beside the Lee to Cromford road had a particularly sinister reputation for taking lives because of a water demon named Crooker who masqueraded as an ash tree. The story begins:

Anyone who walks our country lanes at night knows there are some that are best avoided. Unfriendly things brood in these quiet, lonely places and although safe by day, or unreachable when racing by in the warm security of a car, by night it's different. At night, on foot, a traveller goes in peril of his life, and who knows, maybe his very soul. Such a place is the narrow country road that runs between Lea and Cromford, by the swift and dangerous River Derwent. Travellers in the old days lost their way and wandered from the road to their deaths in the flooded Derwent. Some said it was the river that took them and disfigured their lifeless bodies, for they were terribly disfigured when the waters gave them up. Others said it was the evil work of Crooker, who lurked in the darkest places, waiting, waiting, waiting.

Moorland Fiends

There have been reports of monsters associated with the Pennine hills for thousands of years. Viking invaders considered the place to be haunted by the apparition of a small, squat creature called 'the troll'. The remnant of these old beliefs remains in place-names like Troller's Ghyll near Appletreewick.

Medieval folks believed in the barguest, boggart or boggard, a derivation of 'burgh gaist' or 'borough spirit' in old English. Sightings were reported so regularly in some areas that they acquired names like Boggart Hole at Clough, a wooded dell between Manchester and Oldham, and Boggard Lane between Sheffield and Stocksbridge.

The boggart was a nasty type of ghost, fearsome to behold, with animal features, sharp yellow teeth, shaggy hair and a tail. Their shape was largely perceived, not seen, behind glowing red lights, assumed to be eyes and they had nasty habits like pinching, slapping, kicking and throwing stones (see the story of the Stanbark Boggart on page 36).

The idea of fearsome beasts and wild men lurking in forests and dark, deserted places is echoed in many tales from ancient mythology. They have found their way into old churches as a form of church iconography, and more than 600 years ago, medieval craftsmen were carving hideous creatures into benches, walls, roofs and fonts. Historians tell us that these and the nightmarish gargoyles high up on exterior walls were fashioned by superstitious artisans in the belief that they would frighten away evil spirits.

The Gargoyle that Came Alive

It is hard to imagine anything more grotesque than those carved stone figures we call 'gargoyles' that adorn countless churches and other buildings around the world to drain rain water from the gutters. They tend to sit on their haunches on the parapet of buildings projecting out several feet so that the water is spouted out well clear of the base of the building. Perched up there, they seem quite harmless, and after the introduction of the lead water pipe in the sixteenth century, quite useless, but many are supposed to come alive at night and fly around.

Above and right: *Medieval craftsmen carved these hideous stone heads and fearsome wooden beasts to decorate churches. (Bakewell Church)*

Below: *Gargoyles, like these, were used to frighten away evil spirits and project rain water away from the footings of the building.*

According to one report, a man was walking home through Derby late one night when, out of the corner of his eye, he caught a movement of something flying high above him. It was too big for a bat and too dark for an owl and as the mystery creature landed on the pavement ahead of him, to his horror, he realised that he was surveying something that could only be described as gargoyle-like in appearance. The face was leathery, the set of its eyes were hollow and unblinking, and the mouth agape with fanged teeth. Its wings remained half-spread before it sprang upwards and disappeared. The following day while walking past St Michael's Church, he looked up and there on each of the four corners was a gargoyle: a lion, an angel, a bull and an eagle that looked remarkably like the creature he had seen the previous night.

The Devil and the Dragon

Hob Hurst House is often confused with Thirst House – from the Old English *thyrs* meaning a giant, a demon or even the Devil himself. This was the primeval enemy, the scapegoat for human nature and the source of all evil.

This mythical demon was known by other names like Satan, Lucifer, the Evil One, His Satanic Majesty, Mephistopheles and Old Nick – Nik being a title of the pagan English god Woden. Even the great god Pan, horned and cloven-hoofed, became the conventional Christian Devil; that's where our word 'panic' comes from. The Devil was blamed for all manner of things. It was thought that if a person was ill, he was possessed by the Devil, as illness was brought about by little devils or demons that entered the body.

The Devil was alleged to be bigger and stronger than humans and often used magic spells or curses to do harm, so only the bravest heroes, or a person helped by the gods, could defeat it. This symbol of evil had to be perceived as everything hideous, a monster that lived in wild, lonely places, far away from human towns and villages. It lurked in the harsh menacing landscape of uncharted moors, swamps, lakes and caves. It prowled around anywhere where the spirits of the dead were believed to dwell, and guarded burial mounds and barrows which often contained buried treasures. The thought of the Devil zealously guarding these places was a safeguard to keep intruders at bay.

This manifestation of the Devil had to have the most hideous appearance imaginable but described in a way that was familiar to the popular culture of the day. Its most common guise was as a fearsome dragon that probably evolved from the prehistoric saurian (lizard) mated with other animals. It might have the body of a snake, the head of a lion, lizard's legs, eagle's claws and the tail of a crocodile or scorpion. It's impressive fire-blowing ability was the result of its descendence from the giant water snake, a watery ancestry that made it immune to fire.

It was portrayed with huge wings made of a leathery skin like the wings of a bat, enabling him to rise magically into the air despite its heavy, scaly body and long tail. In the world of fantastic animals the dragon is unique. No other imaginary animal has appeared in so many forms. Yes, it was certainly the result of numerous botched

The Devil was portrayed in many guises.

matings, and if that wasn't scary enough, it had an insatiable taste for humans as sexual partners, food or both.

Until the seventeenth century, scholars wrote of dragons as if they were actual, scientific fact, their anatomy and natural history being recorded in painstaking detail. It is rather disappointing that when the natural world was thoroughly explored in the nineteenth century, no truly awe-inspiring dragons were brought to life. Like other fantasy specimens, they were tossed into the cauldron of fiction, but like the mighty dinosaurs before them, could they have fallen on hard times? Could these monsters of the imagination be rampaging reptiles as alive and authentic as anything that slides, slithers, swims or soars through the grim world of reality?

Devil Names

The Devil takes the form of a dragon when he appears in many local legends. One legend is that Wharncliffe Crags on the Edge of the Peak National Park near Sheffield was once home to a fearsome, fire-breathing dragon that was trampling the trees, munching the milk cows and generally pestering the populace. A local squire named More of More Hall decided to do something about it so he went to Sheffield to commission a suit of armour bristling with steel spikes 6in long. The spiky suit rendered More invulnerable but the dragon's great scalloped scales were simply impregnable, until finally More gave him a kick up the rear and with a shriek of embarrassment the creature expired. The More family crest still displays the dragon symbol.

Could dragons, those monsters of the imagination, still be alive?

Knotlow, a conical hill near Wormhill, west of Tideswell, once housed fire-breathing dragons that terrified the populous and ravaged the countryside. The ancient church at Wormhill is dedicated to St Margaret, who according to legend, was swallowed by a dragon. But quick-thinking Margaret did not despair. She made the sign of the cross, the most holy Christian symbol, and miraculously the dragon split open and Margaret stepped out of its swollen stomach. Dedicating the church to St Margaret was probably rather apt when Wormhill, as its name would suggest, was once believed to be the hillside home of an undesirable creature.

The church in the historical village of Hathersage (written Hereseige in 1086) is dedicated to the dragon-slaying St Michael. The hillside site where the church now stands was probably sacred before the arrival of the first Christian missionaries in the Hope Valley.

Phantom Creatures that Haunt the Peak District

The Devil was thought to have an army of helpers, the most powerful being the foul-smelling, black, short, hairy, ugly-faced Bogies. Not only did these unpleasant spirits do evil deeds against mankind, they had a preference for haunting children. The Boggie man probably got his name from the Middle English word *bogge*, meaning terror – thus naughty children were threatened that if they didn't behave, the boggie man would get them. And just to make things even scarier there was the bug-bear: a boggie man that took the shape of a bear in order to devour his victims.

Such stories have fired the imagination of countless generations of Peakland folk, yet every year people still report encounters with mysterious creatures. Many are considered suspect because there is no photographic evidence or bodies, yet can we dismiss them entirely?

Winged Cats

Read this article reported in the *High Peak News* on 16 June 1897 and judge for yourself whether this is fact or fantasy:

EXTRAORDINARY CAPTURE AT WINSTER — A TOM-CAT WITH WINGS

The most interesting item in natural history, so far as the Matlock district is concerned, transpired this morning, our reporter learns from Mr Roper of Winster, while on Brown Edge, near that village, Mr Roper shot what he thought to be a fox which had been seen in the locality some time previously on Mr Foxlow's land. Thinking he had missed his aim, Mr Roper gave up the quest, but returning later, he found he had killed the animal. It proved to be an extraordinarily large tom-cat, tortoiseshell in colour, with fur two inches and a half long. But what made it remarkable were the remarkable addition of fully-formed pheasant wings projecting from each side of its fourth rib. The animal was exhibited all round the area, but the weather being hot, it began to putrefy and was buried. People who had seen it said that when running the animal used its wings outstretched to help it cover the ground at a tremendous pace.

Winged cats would normally be dismissed as some fantasy animal confined to folklore and 'silly season' tabloid stories were it not for the remarkable fact that they are unquestionably real. In the early 1990s British cryptozoologist Dr Karl Shuker discovered that some cats exhibit a little-known genetic disorder known as feline cutaneous asthenia (FCA) which makes the skin extremely stretchable, especially on the back, haunches and shoulders. These extensions often contain muscle fibres which allows them to be raised and lowered just like wings.

So next time you hear about flying cats, don't dismiss them as a product of some over-active imagination; they are alive and authentic and indisputably living in the Peak District.

The Shuck

Up and down the country demonic black dogs are the most frequently sighted ghostly animals, believed to be monsters from beyond the grave and omens of bad luck that presage death. They are reported so frequently that they have regional names like Barguest, Trash, Tach, Padfoot, Shriker, Old Shock, Shock and in Derbyshire – Shuck. This comes from the Anglo-Saxon word *scucca*, meaning demon. At Crich near Matlock there is a Shuckwood, Shuckstone Lane and Shuckstone field, although only the base of Shuckstone Cross remains on the hilltop above Lea.

According to the *Daily Express* dated October 1925, Edale was terrorised by one such creature of enormous size, black in colour and possessing a howl like a fog-horn. One eyewitness is reported as saying, 'It sat on its haunches and it was bigger than me.'

People who have seen the shuck describe it as a huge, shaggy black animal with fiery eyes as big as saucers, backward-pointing feet and a stream of sulphurous vapour pouring from its throat. There is the smell of brimstone and burning where it has roamed. If you should meet one, don't strike it, because like a ball of energy, it will ignite. The driver of a wagon struck out at one that exploded, setting him and his wagon on fire. A horseman struck one with his riding crop, at which point, it exploded in a flash, blowing the rider off his horse and the clothes off his back. The traumatised horse was eventually found two days later. A farmhand was leading two carthorses along a country lane early one morning, when a large shaggy, black animal came paddling down the lane towards them. The boy and horses froze in their tracks as the creature passed through a hedge and disappeared in a flash of white light.

A lorry driver and his mate were driving along a rural road when out of the bushes came a huge black dog-like creature. It seemed oblivious to the lorry and strolled across the road, causing the driver to brake suddenly, then it turned its head and both men stared in disbelief. The animal was like a silhouette with no features; no nose, mouth or eyes, then suddenly it just disappeared.

Phantom creatures are said to haunt the Peak District.

A miner and his mate were returning home one moonlit evening when the miner was terrified by the sudden appearance of a shuck, although surprisingly only he could see it. He was so convinced that the dog was an omen of bad luck he refused to go down the mine the following day. His disbelieving colleague did and was killed when the roof fell on him.

Phantom Protector

Just to show that not all phantom dogs are evil, here are two stories of phantom protectors. A young woman was travelling on foot in a remote country area late one night. There was no street lighting or pavements and the hedges and overhanging trees formed strange shapes and made even stranger noises as she hurried past. Her imagination was playing tricks and she was quaking with fear as she almost ran headlong into a large, black dog that seemed to appear from nowhere. Although usually afraid of dogs, she found this one to be friendly and comforting and it stayed with her until the lights of houses were reached when, with a wag of its tail, it went its own way, disconcertingly disappearing through a solid stone wall.

Along the road from Calver Sough to Stoney Middleton, a Methodist minister was walking one night when he realised he was being followed. He was carrying the collection money from the various chapels he served and he felt rather vulnerable until he was unexpectedly joined by a large dog that stayed protectively by his heels until he reached his destination. Reaching down to pat the dog, his hand passed straight through it.

three

ROAD AND RAIL FRIGHTS

Crossroads Ghosts

The point where roads intersect has long been associated with magic and evil. Hecate, the Greek goddess of witchcraft, was also goddess of crossroads and animals were sacrificed to her there. Witches were alleged to gather at crossroads in order to conjure up the Devil and his demons, and practice black magic. Some spells were considered to be more effective if they were cast at a cross roads. The evil reputation of crossroads was enhanced by the fact that it was often the site of the local gallows. The bodies of undesirables like murderers, suicides, criminals and convicted vampires were habitually buried at crossroads, often with a stake through their heart to stop them haunting. The reason for crossroad burials appears to differ but some say it was to show the persons marginal position in society, or because no parish would acknowledge them or because the ghost of the deceased would be unable to decide which road to get back home.

The Stocksbridge bypass is the scene of many paranormal happenings.

The Disjointed Ghost at the Crossroads

One evening in March, a car containing four women was travelling on the B6036 between Ashover and Woolley Moor. It was about 8 p.m. The night was dark and visibility poor on the unlit country road, but on the stretch overlooking Ogston reservoir, they encountered a small, headless figure, dressed in an off-white smock. There was only the outline of a head and it was waving its arms around disjointedly.

The car's occupants panicked and drove off, although they later returned but saw nothing. There has been another sighting of this ghost at almost the same place, so perhaps this is what is known as a recording-type ghost, caused by some extreme emotion at the time, but what exactly triggers the replay is unclear.

The Haunting History of Hanging Bridge

Hanging Bridge is on the Derbyshire/Staffordshire border, but names like Hanging Bridge and Gallows Tree Lane, which drops down to the bridge, will always act as a reminder of the area's gruesome past. In 1745, when Bonnie Prince Charlie made his futile attempt to re-gain the crown for his father, many of his Jacobite soldiers and supporters were captured by the English and executed in this area. Apparently some still linger there. Locals believe Hanging Bridge is a place where evil spirits meet and it has certainly had its fair share of accidents and ghostly sightings including a headless man and a ghost who is seen leaping off the bridge.

The Phantom Children at Stocksbridge Bypass

During 1987-88 while construction work was being carried out on the Stocksbridge bypass, John Holmes was employed at a lorry depot immediately below the bypass. When working nights he and his colleagues often had the feeling of being watched, but the most bizarre experience first happened one freezing cold night while John was busy working. He paused to listen to the sound of a group of small voices singing. He could not work out the song which seemed to be coming from nearby, but it sounded very spooky. Over a period of time, it would continue on and off until the early hours.

In 1987 two security guards named Steven Brookes and David Goldthorpe were employed by Constant Securities to patrol the unfinished bypass. On 7 September 1987 they were patrolling Pearoyd Lane, one of the ancient moorland roads, which was being disturbed by the building work. They were near Pearoyd Bridge, which carried a narrow flyover above the route of the bypass, when they saw what they later described as a group of young children in medieval clothing dancing round a pylon. They stopped their vehicle and got out to investigate, but the children had gone and despite a thorough search there was no sign of their footprints in the soft ground.

There have been many other witnesses to this sight. In March 1995, childminder Ms Pat Heathcote corroborated the story. She watched about eight children dancing around what seemed like an invisible maypole on a grass mound near the new bridge.

Three weeks later, Ms Barbara Lee of the Midhopestones Arms saw them playing in a field above the new bridge, miles away from where children usually play. She described them as dancing happily together. The girls wore shin-length skirts, white pinafores and mob caps, and the boys wore breeches.

The Monk on Stocksbridge Bypass

Traffic police who patrol the notoriously dangerous Stocksbridge bypass attribute the high accident rate to problems associated with many other newly opened roads, but ignore any association with the past, and the fact that the area is rich in local folklore.

A phantom monk haunts the area.

Many years before the bypass was even considered, Annie Staniforth, who lived at a cottage at White Row Farm, Hunshelf, near the route of the road, confided to her daughter that she had often seen a ghostly monk. The stories were passed on to her daughter Ms Katrina Hewitt, who, as a child was told that a monk was killed by soldiers in the vicinity and still wanders the moors trying to find peace. More recently, an old legend has been discovered which relates to a monk who lived at Hunshelf Hall. His last wish was to be buried at nearby Stannington, but this was ignored and he was buried in unhallowed ground. The result of this was that he haunted the area, but since the motorway construction, his sightings seem to have been more regular, which would indicate that his final resting place has in fact been disturbed. The monk is one of the spectres that paranormal researchers claim now haunts the road, alongside the eerie feelings, dark figures, and musty smells that are regularly reported.

Another sighting made by Steven Brookes and David Goldthorpe as they patrolled the unfinished bypass was a man standing on the newly-constructed Pearoyd Bridge. Not sure whether this was a practical joker or a suicide attempt and unable to reach the bridge from their position below, Brookes stayed at the base of the bridge while Goldthorpe drove round behind the figure. As he swung the vehicle round and directed full headlights at the figure wrapped in a long, dark cloak, both men stared in stunned disbelief because the figure had no head and the light passed straight through his body. Within seconds it had gone completely. Both men were so shocked by this experience they informed the police and visited a local priest asking for the place to be exorcised.

The local police decided to investigate, so four days later, at midnight on Friday 11 September 1987, PC Dick Ellis and SC John Beet visited the bypass. Both men were serious, no nonsense officers. They drove onto the unfinished road and although the lights from the steelworks below reflected upon the bridge, everywhere was pitch black. They parked their patrol car and sat for a while admiring the clear sky and full moon. Ellis put down his window, and then suddenly just froze. Out of the corner of his eye, he saw someone standing by the side of the car, but as he turned quickly round, there was nothing there. Suddenly Beet let out a scream. The figure was standing at his side of the car and he described him as looking rather Dickensian, from the 1820s era. As he tried to focus more clearly, the figure disappeared.

Assuming it was a joker, both men leapt out of the patrol car and searched the area but found nothing. They got back into the car and drove towards the bridge. There they parked, with the intention of using the radio to call for assistance but suddenly the patrol car began to rock and was jolted by a series of loud thumps as if something was impacting upon the boot. This proved to be just too much and the terrified officers turned their car round and headed back to safety.

Later when interviewed for the Michael Aspel television programme *Strange But True*, PC Ellis said it was impossible to dismiss it as imagination when both he and his colleague had experienced the same thing, and anyway, the police don't make up those kind of stories.

During the winter of 1987, while the bypass was under construction, Chapeltown resident Graham Brooke and his son Nigel were out jogging. As they approached a lay-by on the road towards Wortley village, they noticed a figure dressed in a cape and hood walking with his back towards the traffic. It was dusk but not dark and as the man walked towards them, he was so clear, they could see his blank face and count the buttons that fastened his dark-brown cape. He carried a bag attached to a chain. They could hear the chain rattling along the ground and they could also smell a very fusty odour, but Graham realised in amazement that the man was walking in the ground rather than on the surface. As they stood in stunned horror, the lights of a lorry swept the area and the spectre had disappeared.

In 1990, lorry driver Melbourne Heptinstall had just pulled into the trailer park on Station Road, Deepcar. He was busy untying the ropes fastened to his trailer, when he gave a sudden shiver. It was as if a cold breeze had enveloped him and he could smell a rather fusty odour. Looking up he saw what he described as a monk-like figure gliding through his headlights.

In July 1990, Judy Simpson and her husband David were travelling along the B6088 at the village of Wortley, adjacent to the haunted highway, when over to their left they saw the grey outline of a figure that seemed oblivious to the road and ran in front of their car. As Judy slammed on the brakes, the figure just seemed to melt into the car and disappear. Thoroughly shocked, they got out of the car and looked around but there was nothing.

Sightings of the monk and other mysterious dark presences associated with this stretch of road are collected by psychic consultant Lucinda Beevers of Peniston. She encountered the apparition herself while driving home via the bypass. Being used to dealing with the paranormal, when a dark shape appeared next to her in her car, she quickly recited the Lord's Prayer, and it vanished. The figure which she described as large and very frightening was such a sudden and unnerving encounter that Lucinda is convinced others must have had the same experience. On one occasion, Lucinda saw the shadowy figure appear in someone else's car ahead of her. When she overtook the car, the shape vanished. There have been so many horrendous accidents on this stretch that it could be responsible for the high accident rate.

Most of the sightings are around Pearoyd Lane and the adjacent bridge, but people have encountered the frightening presence and the figure of the monk over a much wider area and over a three-mile stretch of the motorway. Lucinda has obtained testimonies from at least fifteen people who have reported picking out the figure in their headlights, and either seeing or sensing the presence in their cars. Following their encounters, many needed counselling.

On New Year's Eve 1997, Paul Ford and his wife Jane were in their car driving along the Stocksbridge bypass towards Stocksbridge when Paul noticed a figure in the middle of the road. At first glance it looked like some idiot trying to cross the busy road, then as Paul stared in horror and slammed on the brakes, he realized that the figure dressed in a long cloak had no face and was hovering above the road. As with the majority of these witnesses, he knew nothing about the previous claims of a wandering monk.

According to Lucinder Beever, although the spectral figure of the monk instils fear in people, it is not an evil spirit, just a very troubled one. Several mediums claim to have helped the spirit to pass to the spirit world, so perhaps the ghostly monk of the Stocksbridge bypass has at last been helped to pass to the next stage of being.

The Phantom Hitch-Hiker

It was a cold winter night and a young courting couple were riding a motor bike and sidecar along the road between The Fox House and Sheffield when they stopped to offer a lift to a hitchhiker who seemed in distress. She was obviously a biker, dressed in motorcycling leathers and a crash helmet, but apart from giving a Sheffield address, she said nothing. She climbed onto the pillion seat and they set off.

They hadn't gone very far when to their horror, the couple realised that the girl biker had disappeared. Totally mystified, they retraced their route back to Fox House, but the girl had simply vanished. They were so shaken they reported the incident to the police and then decided to go to the address given them by the girl.

The door was opened by a middle-aged woman and the couple tried to explain in a rather apologetic manner what had happened. The woman burst into tears. The description of the hitchhiker fitted perfectly that of their daughter who had been killed in a recent motor-bike accident on the very spot where the couple had first seen her.

The road between The Fox House and Sheffield, where a couple offered a lift to a phantom hitch-hiker.

The Replayed Road Accident

One night, a police dog-handler was driving along the road heading towards Pilsley when a figure appeared in the full beam of the headlights. Although the officer braked furiously he couldn't avoid hitting him head on. The man bounced over the bonnet and fell. In a state of shock, the officer grabbed a torch and jumped out of his van. He released his dog who jumped out, howled pitifully and shot off down the road.

The officer searched the roadside looking for the accident victim but there was no one and the hedge was undisturbed. He checked the front of the vehicle for signs of the impact, but could see nothing. He got back inside the van and proceeded slowly down the road just to make sure the injured person hadn't somehow stumbled away from the scene of the accident. As he drove he realised that although he had seen the impact he hadn't felt it or heard it.

At first light, he returned to the scene of the accident but could find no trace of anything strange. Back at the police station, he began to explain what had happened but the sergeant stopped him. 'Don't worry about it,' he said. 'A man was killed at that spot many years ago and the replay is witnessed regularly.'

The Lonely Old Farmer and the Headless Cow

A man regularly drove along the A619 road from Baslow to Bakewell and on many occasions saw an old man leaning on a five-bar gate, smoking a pipe. This same old man seemed to appear so frequently that it became much more than just a coincidence. He was a ghost, and in death it would appear that this old farmer was doing what he had done in his lifetime.

There is another story that relates to a five-bar gate, this time located somewhere in the countryside near Taddington, just south of Buxton. Should you be driving around there, keep your eyes open for a headless cow. The story is that the poor beast got its head stuck in a five bar gate and try as they might, no one could get the beast's head free. Finally, the farmer made a decision. The gate was worth more than the cow, so his head was sawn off. No wonder the poor distressed animal haunts the place.

The Cows that were Abducted

Police officer Alan Godfrey was on Burnley Road, Todmorton just after 5 a.m. looking for some lost cattle. There had been reports that they had been seen from a nearby housing estate and although patrols had looked for them, the cows seemed to have temporarily vanished. The farmer was mystified as to how they had escaped, but what was more surprising was that they turned up at dawn in a field that seemed almost inaccessible. The question was how had they moved themselves?

The field where they were found was extremely muddy because it had rained heavily during the night, yet there were no hoof prints to indicate how these heavy animals had reached the place where they now stood. It was almost as if they had been picked up and relocated into another field a few hundred yards away across what has become known as a haunted road.

This is not the only incident of what have been dubbed 'alien abductions.' On 28 November 1980, a few hundred yards away from this very spot, police officer Alan Godfrey reported experiencing a swirling grey mist and being apparently sucked up into some kind of spatial and temporal anomaly. Coming to his senses he found himself 'relocated' further down the road without any memory of the transition. Several minutes were unaccounted for. Ten months earlier, a truck driver named Bill also reported a similar experience on this same stretch of road and other incidents are regularly reported throughout the Pennines.

Unusual Bombardments

There have been a number of instances of a rock-throwing poltergeist. Stones, bits of iron, and coins have from time to time been reported as crashing down to earth, but the ice bomb is the most common form of falling debris and blamed on the waste systems of aircraft. The Civil Aviation at Manchester Airport confirm that about thirty ice falls per year are reported

But how do we explain the unusual bombardments that occurred in the pre-aeroplane days? The fall of manna in the Bible is backed by a number of historically verified stories of similar falls of organic goo. Sand occasionally rains over parts of Britain and when analysed, it is found to have come all the way from the Sahara desert. It has been sucked up by an atmospheric vortex and then, after drifting across Europe, dropped 2,000 miles away.

The writings of journalist Charles Fort, who collected such oddities from the late nineteenth and early twentieth centuries are full of falling things. The most commonly accepted explanation is that they occur as a result of an atmospheric vortex akin to a whirlwind. This creates a small zone of low gravity that sucks up small creatures and carries them aloft a short distance before depositing them to earth. Is that what happened on 8 July 1841, when fish and ice fell from the skies in Derby?

Curiously this is not the only example. Similar incident involving fish, toads, frogs, crabs and worms have been reported all over Britain. On 9 November 1984 the people of Accrington on the northern edge of the Peak District experienced a new hazard – falling apples. The apples, all of good quality and edible, descended from the air without any visible source; there were no nearby trees. They considered cargo falling out of a plane, yet the deluge lasted for an hour and when counted there were over 300 apples.

Fred Swindon, an industrial officer in Sheffield, was about to drive to work on the morning of 23 February 1981 when he found a small shoal of recently dropped fish covering his car. There were too many to be dropped by a bird, but no other obvious explanation could be found. The fish were about 3in long but not wet or surrounded by water, and still flapping. One fish was kept alive by dropping it into his windscreen wiper water-bottle. When analysed it was decided that the fish were local, probably from a nearby river, but how they had dropped from the sky in this way remains a mystery.

The Ghost of Spend Lane

So many accidents have happened on Spend Lane, north of Ashbourne that it is known as an accident black-spot, but many believe the lane to be haunted.

In 1955, a car carrying a party of wedding guests crashed into a ditch on Spend Land. At precisely the same moment the top tier fell off the wedding cake at the reception.

In 1977, a car travelling along Spend Lane was suddenly filled with a tremendous wind, even though all the windows were tightly closed. There was the sound of upholstery ripping although the only damage found was a metal disc that had been torn off the dashboard.

In another incident on the lane, a girl was thrown by a normally well-behaved horse.

So what links these three incidents? It is widely believed that they are all connected with the story of a bride killed on her wedding day. Apparently, the bride was travelling

Paranormal activity on Spend Lane can be traced back to the time when a bridal carriage overturned, killing the bride.

along Spend Lane from Fenny Bentley to her wedding in Ashbourne, but tragically, her carriage turned over and she was killed.

The Phantom Cyclist

Two men were walking up Eyam Dale one morning after an early-morning rabbit-shoot when they had to leap hurriedly aside to avoid being run over by a cyclist racing down the steep gradient. Turning to curse the cyclist, the men were shocked to see that the road was completely deserted.

Down this same stretch of road one dark night, a man was walking home when he distinctly heard the swish of the rubber tyres and the ringing of a bicycle bell. He turned to stare in the direction of the noise but could see nothing.

'What idiot is riding down here without lights?' he muttered to himself as he stepped aside but the cyclist never materialised.

A man and his wife were walking along Stoney Middleton Dale when they heard a cyclist approaching from behind. They instinctively stepped to the side to let it pass just as a Chesterfield service bus approached from the opposite direction. The bus rounded a bend and swept the road with its headlights and there was no sign of a cyclist.

The phantom cyclist was actually seen by a keen cyclist as he laboriously climbed the ascent of Eyam Dale one very wet day. Dripping with water and making hard work of the climb, the cyclist was amazed to see another cyclist effortlessly overtake him and pull away. Not only that, the phantom cyclist was bone dry despite the fact that it was pouring with rain.

What the Cyclist Saw

An isolated incident experienced by another cyclist happened near Carsington. The man had been helping with the milking at Ouslow Farm one Saturday afternoon and was cycling back home to Carsington in the darkness. His cycle was equipped with a carbide lamp which penetrated the darkness, illuminating the road and the verge either side, but as he reached Ouslow Hollow, he instinctively jammed on his brakes to avoid colliding with a woman who was crossing the road.

She seemed to have come through a solid thorn hedge, glide across the road and straight through the opposite hedge. Trembling with disbelief, he mounted his bike and peddled as fast as he could, but back home, he was able to describe the figure in accurate detail. She was middle aged and wearing a dark, full-skirted dress with tight bodice, high collar and short cape. On her head was a close-fitting hat.

The man told this story to Mr Frank Radford of Brassington who borrowed a book on period costume from the local library. Without hesitation, the man picked out a costume fashionable during the late Victorian and early Edwardian period, dating the phantom lady to around 1900, but who she was remains a mystery.

The Disappearing Horse

Mabel Dickinson and her friend Frances Smith were walking along the Hathersage to Bamford road. They had reached an area known as Sicklehome Hollow when Frances pointed out a white horse in the field. Mabel looked where Frances was pointing but could see nothing and there were no horses anywhere around. Mabel tried to convince Frances that it was a trick of the light, but she was equally adamant that there was definitely a horse in the field. The argument was settled when they both heard a ghostly neigh and according to Frances, the horse simply disappeared.

Rowsley Railway Station Goes Back in Time

A group of paranormal experts are trying to prove whether or not Rowsley station is haunted. The Society for Paranormal Research, a national group, has also visited Darley Dale station after a number of ghosts were spotted.

The ghostly figure of a soldier is said to haunt Rowsley and a fireman is said to haunt the sheds at Darley Dale station.

After his visit to Rowsley, Jack Phillips, vice president of the Society for Paranormal Research said, 'This is absolutely fantastic. Suffice to say there was enough going on for us to arrange to go back. It's the strangest place I have ever been to in twenty years of paranormal investigation.'

The group managed to gain photographic evidence of strange phenomena and audio recordings of voices answering questions. In addition, Mr Phillips claims the group heard the sound of a steam train thundering along track that has not been used for years.

Jackie Statham, managing director for Peak Rail said:

> In Darley Dale there has always been the story of a woman who committed suicide on the railway line. I've looked into some records but I've not found any evidence.
>
> We have the 1940s weekend every year and last year members of the paranormal group saw a soldier walking down the track. It had gone midnight and they thought it was a person in costume, but when they got closer, he just vanished.

The group used a professional medium to help with their investigation and coincided their Saturday-night researches with a 1940s weekend which was happening at Darley Dale.

Mr Phillips believes the nostalgia weekend was a good opportunity for a time-slip. He said, 'This is when everything goes blurred and you're transported back in time for a few seconds. It's you who appears as a ghost in another time.'

The group use trigger objects to stimulate the appearance of ghosts. Mr Phillips said, 'trigger objects can be anything relevant. For example if we are dealing with a child we may place a toy.' He added, 'As a parapsychologist I wouldn't say there is a ghost, but I am satisfied that Rowsley train station is paranormally active. It is definitely worthy of further investigation.'

Steam trains and nostalgia may have prompted paranormal activity at Darley Dale station.

Twelve Headless Men on Shady Lane

Shady Lane is a rather lonely stretch of road which runs between Great Longstone and Ashford in the Water, but supposedly if you travel along there at dusk or dawn you may just encounter twelve men carrying a coffin. On closer inspection you will see that the men are headless and the coffin empty, apparently intended for the unfortunate person who meets this strange funeral cortège.

However, take heart, I'm assured that people have seen this strange procession and lived to tell the tale. If the funeral cortège are walking towards you it means you will be scooped up into the coffin, but if they are walking away, you will be fine. I'm not sure what would happen if you made the split-second decision to turn and run, which would surely be the most obvious solution!

The Peddler at Darley Dale

At Darley Dale, before you pass the railway station, the road to the left is Church Lane. In the seventeenth century, it was known as Ghost Lane. The ghost was a Scottish peddler who was robbed and murdered here. His ghost is seen near the large sycamore tree 150yds from the churchyard, where you will find the largest yew in England, reckoned to be 2,000 years old.

Shady Lane where you might encounter twelve headless men carrying a coffin.

Ghost Lane, Darley Dale, where a murdered peddler is seen.

The High Peak Carter

The Pennines have long been associated with strange phenomena. Curious hovering lights, strange buzzing noises and even phantom aircraft are regularly reported. Baffling though these are, imagine the surprise of drivers on the A57 (where it meets the A6013 from Bamford) having to brake sharply as they suddenly find themselves behind a carter and his horse. This is a true country rustic, the type you would meet regularly in this area a hundred or so years ago when this wild, inhospitable country was inhabited by lead miners and hill farmers. People who have seen him describe this apparition as a carter wearing a tall hat, knee-length smock and carrying a long riding whip. He is walking along at a steady pace leading a horse and a strange cart with high sides. A motorcyclist who saw him said he disappeared in the blink of an eye.

Something Dark and Evil

The hairpin bend in the Glossop to Woodhead road above Ogden and Torside Clough is known as the Devil's Elbow and refers to the tale of the Devil pursuing a young couple. When almost within reach of the girl, the Devil was thwarted by a strange burning light which froze his arm and allowed the lovers to escape.

The area is still linked with strange activity and many people report seeing odd lights, but one night during the 1950s John Davies, a railway signalman, was returning home to Woodhead on his motorcycle and experienced something totally different.

The evening sky was illuminated by a full-harvest moon and for some reason John decided to stop and pull over to the side of the road. He then described how he had seen a peculiar shape like a huge black slug that slid across the road up the wall and disappeared. As it slid it made a peculiar gritty noise similar to that made by feet on wet gravel. 'It looked like it was swimming across the road,' said John, who got off his bike to get a closer look:

> It had the head of a whale and a white eye with a black pupil going round and round. It went right up the wall and disappeared and I got off my bike and went to have a look but it had gone. I've been over there thousands of times but never seen anything like it before or since.

Although no one else has reported seeing this huge black slug, walkers in the area often get a feeling of being followed by something dark and evil. They are usually too frightened to turn and see what it is and opt to get away as soon as possible.

The Doctor and the Devil

Devil's Dyke on the Bleaklow side of the moors gets its name from an old tale that bears a distinct similarity to the eighteenth-century tale of Tam O'Shanter by Robbie Burns. The Peak District version tells how a doctor was called out one night to visit a sick patient living in the heart of the country. On his way home he had the distinct impression that he was being followed and to his horror discovered it to be by the Devil himself. He urged his horse into a gallop knowing that the only way he could escape the Devil's grasp was to cross running water, and a stream lay ahead. Rivers and streams are boundaries that the Devil can't cross.

Just as the doctor reached the safety of the stream, the Devil reached out and grabbed his horse's tail, but it withered at his touch.

They say that the Devil was so angry at being robbed of possessing the doctor's soul, he scratched out a deep gully with his talons, a feature that can still be seen today.

Henry Columbell's Fruitless Search

On the night of the first full moon in March, echoes of a 400-year-old tragedy resound above Darley Hillside as a phantom horseman sets off on a desperate search for his wife and family.

Back in the seventeenth century, Henry Columbell, his wife Jane and their two young children were returning to the Columbell ancestral home at Darley Nether Hall after their annual seasonal visit to Eckington, where they had been staying at Jane's father's home.

Escorted by only three servants, the little cavalcade was faced with mile after mile of stony, muddy tracks, and the going was especially slow as Jane was in the latter stages of pregnancy and being carried in a horse litter. Henry rode beside the litter, and their two small children were being carried in the arms of menservants.

As the day wore on, sleet began to fall and the skies turned dark, but the small group eventually reached the Chesterfield home of a relative where they spent the night.

The next day the party made steady progress as they began their arduous climb towards Wadshelf and the open moors above Holymoorside. All around them stretched an endless expanse of open moorland with no shelter against the biting winds that blew across the desolate wasteland. It was a cold, tiring journey but worse was to come because dark storm clouds were gathering in the distance. Bad weather was approaching and they were in the middle of nowhere. To return to their Chesterfield kin would take almost as long as to go on but they would soon be in dire need of help. Henry knew that if he rode fast he could reach Darley Nether Hall and return with more men and provisions before nightfall, so taking just one man-servant, he set off at a desperate gallop, leaving his family with two menservants to struggle on.

The snowstorm broke before Henry Columbell even reached Darley Nether Hall, sweeping in on a furious blizzard that showed no sign of abating. Henry's attempts to return for his family brought the horses to the ground and for three long days every attempt at rescue was thwarted by the blizzard that raged day and night. Finally they were able to set off battling against huge snow-drifts but to no avail. They searched in vain and Henry was utterly distraught when the bodies of his beloved wife and children were eventually found huddled together in a hollow in the middle of the exposed moors.

The tragedy broke his heart and stole his reason. From then on until his death four years later, he would gallop over the moors on moonlit nights calling his wife's name in his desperate search, and his ghost continues to do exactly the same.

Darley Nether Hall fell into ruins and was eventually pulled down in 1776, but the family coat of arms can still be seen on a plaque inside the Columbell Quire in St Helen's Church, Darley, where their bodies were laid to rest. And if you should be on the bleak, open moorlands of Beeley Moors round Farley and Darley hillside on the first night of the full moon in March, you might even encounter the ghost of Henry Columbell as he gallops by in his fruitless search.

The Phantom Horse in Spooky Woods

Back in 1947, a group of teenagers decided to camp in a small wood south-west of Stocksbridge which had acquired the name 'Spooky Woods.'

It was getting late. They had damped down their camp fire and had retired to their tents when they heard the unmistakable sound of a horse galloping towards them. As it came nearer and nearer, the petrified campers realised that it was coming straight towards them and they really expected to be trampled to death, then suddenly it just stopped. There was no sound of it changing directions or turning round. The campers went outside to investigate and found no hoof marks in the soft earth. They were so spooked they ran to the nearest farm-house. They had heard the sound of a horse that wasn't there or, more likely, the sound of a horse that had once been there. The whole experience had been very real.

The Headless Horseman

A headless horseman patrols the moors north-east of Leek in the area of Butterton Moor between Onecote and Warslow. In 1930, a villager met this awesome spectre at a crossroads and afterwards announced, 'it was a man on a white horse without a head on, an awful gory sight.'

He was luckier than a Warslow man on his way to Leek market who was snatched up by the demon rider and rode behind him as they galloped at a fearsome speed across the countryside. They sped over fields and jumped stone walls, and then eventually the man's battered body was found on his own doorstep. He died shortly afterwards, but whether from his injuries or delayed shock is uncertain.

The Haunts of Dick Turpin

The highwayman is often portrayed as a romantic figure attired in fancy clothes, an aristocrat amongst thieves who just happens to be down on his luck. This dashing young gentleman would ride around the country righting wrongs and stealing nothing

Does Dick Turpin's ghost haunt the Peacock Inn at Oakerthorpe?

from a pretty maid but a kiss. That's the romantic image; the mystique that surrounds the highwayman owes much to this supposed chivalry and courage. The archetypal highwayman was born in the aftermath of the Civil War when the execution of Charles I in 1649 left many Royalist officers without any means of support. Because they were unaccustomed to earning a living and had no trade to fall back on, they took to the high road.

By 1705, the year of Dick Turpin's birth, the highwayman was a popular folk hero, especially amongst the poor who had nothing to fear from such a person as they seldom travelled and more importantly had nothing worth stealing.

According to the 1890 Ward's Almanac, Dick Turpin was born in Horsley, Essex but although there are many Turpins living in the area and even more in the graveyard, there is no direct family link. He initially worked as a butcher's apprentice but wanting a more lucrative career, took to stealing cattle and horses. This progressed to smuggling, housebreaking then highway robbery. His reputation was greatly enhanced by his gallantry to ladies, his illicit affairs and his numerous narrow escapes.

Considering his lifestyle, inns were an integral part of his life on the road, and as he travelled through the area on a regular basis, it is steeped in Turpin folklore. Many old inns still exist so it is not surprising that several along his old routes claim to have enjoyed his custom. The Peacock Inn at Oakerthorpe, on the eastern side of the Peak District, is one of them. Dating back to the eleventh century, it lies at the junction of what were three turnpike roads. It became a commercial inn in 1613 and during its heyday as a coaching inn in the eighteenth century it had stabling for seventy-two horses, with sixteen coaches changing horses at the Peacock Inn daily. According to legend, near the blacksmith's forge at the rear of the premises it once possessed a secret underground stable which local horse thieves used. Apparently Dick Turpin also used this stable to hide Black Bess.

The unarmed post-boys who carried the mail on horseback, frequently at night to avoid being held up by slow-moving herds of animals, were a prime target for the highwaymen and robberies were frequent. The post-boys were often suspected of being in league with the highwaymen and the Post Office advised anyone sending bank drafts or valuable documents to cut them in half and send each piece separately.

Dick Turpin was hanged at York on 7 April 1739, but the ghost of the intrepid Dick still haunts many old roads and wayside inns, although his black-clad figure, complete with tricorn hat and cloak slung over his shoulder, is described by witnesses as having no face.

The Highwayman and the Poor Farmer

The Peak District was once frequented by the notorious highwayman John Nevison of Pontefract, also known as Swift Nick. During the late seventeenth century, he was known to go regularly to the ale-houses and inns of the Peak, and one market day he was in the Castle Hotel in Bakewell where he got chatting to a poor tenant farmer from Padley who had just sold some cattle to pay his quarterly rent at Michaelmas. Celebrating his shrewd bargaining with a few strong pints of autumn ale, the farmer was happy to accept more from a friendly stranger who asked him the way to Sheffield. All caution gone, the tipsy farmer told the stranger that the quickest route was past his house and proposed that they should travel together. They'd be company for each other and offer added protection against highwaymen. The well-dressed stranger agreed and they set off from Bakewell as the sun was sinking low.

Taking the Hassop road, they travelled in silence until they reached Calver Sough where they allowed their horses to rest for a few minutes before the next stage of the journey to Tomlin's Gate. The farmer admired the stranger's fine horse to which he replied, 'Aye. It's best to be well mounted when the roads are lonely and robbers are abroad.'

As they rode towards Stoke Hall, under the dark beech trees, the stranger produced a pistol and pressed it to the farmers chest, ordering him to hand over his money.

'Please don't take my money,' sobbed the befuddled farmer. 'I sold my cows to pay the rent at Michaelmas. It's all the money I have in the world, and if you take it I'll be thrown off my farm. I have a wife and family and we'll be paupers if I can't pay.'

John Nevison said nothing, but pressed harder with the pistol, clicking back the hammer as he did so. With a heavy heart, the farmer reached inside his coat and brought out the canvas bag containing the gold.

'If this is indeed the rent money as you say, you shall have it back, you have my word upon that, but I have need of it now and you have ten days till Michaelmas.' As he spoke, Nevison snatched the bag from the farmer and rode off.

The farmer had ten days to lament his lost gold, but as he sat late on the tenth night thinking he'd soon have neither hearth nor home, he heard a horse galloping up from

Travelling through the Peak District has always been hazardous, particularly in the days of highwaymen like the notorious John Nevison.

Grindleford Bridge. Reaching his house, it reigned in briefly and there was a smash as something flew through the window. Lying on the floor amongst the broken glass was a canvas bag and inside was the money Nevison had taken from the farmer, plus an extra guinea wrapped in a scrap of paper. On the paper was written, 'Interest for the loan of rent money.'

John Nevison, Gentleman of the Road, had kept his word, but does he also return to the scene? Many people have reported seeing a rider galloping along this road, although it's also likely that you might encounter a phantom cavalier, a coach or a bobby on a bicycle.

Hassop's Cavalier and Coach

If you travel along the Bakewell to Hassop road, don't be surprised if you encounter a phantom cavalier who supposedly steps out into the road in front of vehicles, or the phantom coach and horses that is likely to overtake you. Could this be speeding away from John Nevison? Many motorists who have encountered them suffer from shock, and apparently one died after swerving to avoid crashing into a coach and horses crossing his path. Traumatized people who have witnessed these strange phenomena call in the Eyre Arms in Hassop to tell their stories, and they all bear a striking similarity.

A phantom coach is often reported passing through Hassop.

What few realise is that the cavalier also haunts the Eyre Arms and has appeared to customers and staff.

Recently I heard an extension to these sightings when early one morning a guest staying at Hassop Hall saw from his bedroom window a coach and horses being driven along the drive. It looked so impressive that when the guest went down for breakfast he asked the receptionist if it was possible to book the coach for a nostalgic drive around the area. The receptionist looked puzzled. It is possible to book a period coach for such an event through Red Horse Stables at Darley Dale, but after making a thorough check, the guest was informed that no such coach had called at Hassop Hall that morning.

The Paralysed Driver at Abney

A carter in his horse-drawn trap made a regular journey along the lane from Leadmill to Abney and on various occasions a phantom figure would appear and take the horse's bridle to lead it for a short way. This did not unduly disturb the driver or freak the horse but the driver's dog would cower in the trap, its hair bristling with fear. One day however, when the phantom appeared, the driver was caught off guard and involuntarily raised his whip. Instantly his arm fell to his side limp and useless, and he never recovered from his paralysis.

The Headless Coachman

The Red Lion, Wirksworth, is a former coaching inn, rebuilt in the eighteenth century, but may date back to medieval times, now haunted by the ghost of a coachman. According to local legend, one day he was trying to manoeuvre his coach through the archway when the horse suddenly bolted and taken by surprise, he was decapitated. Now his headless figure has been seen wandering the premises.

Phantom Coaches

Residual energy from the stage-coach era of the past is regularly experienced today, often in the form of phantom coaches customarily black and pulled by headless black horses. The driver usually has skeletal or grotesque features. They are often driven at a furious pace and are believed to be seen prior to a death in the family. Alternatively of course, it is said that anyone who gets in the way of a phantom coach will be carried away to their own doom!

The road which runs between Youlgreave and Middleton has a phantom coach and horses lit by ghostly lamps and accompanied by ghostly dogs. One witness is said to have felt the wind as it passed.

These phantom coaches pulled by headless, black horses are encountered all over Derbyshire but the Duffield coach is an exception. This nightmarish apparition is a coach pulled by five white horses with fiery eyes and smoking nostrils, being driven at a furious pace along the Valley of the Derwent. Manned by a skeleton coachman and postilions with grotesque features, as it approaches Duffield Bridge, it dashes into the river and disappears.

The Postman and the Carriage

A Brassington postman also kept a few hens at a farm in the vicinity of Longcliffe, so every evening after work, he'd go to the isolated farm to feed and tend his hens. It was getting near to Christmas and the mail was mounting up, so one evening he decided to relieve the following morning's postal delivery by taking some Christmas mail to a few of the isolated farms in the area at the same time. He was just returning through the fields from one isolated farm when he saw a coach and horses coming up the road from the direction of Ashbourne. The coach was brilliantly illuminated and the postman had never seen such a vehicle before, but as it was heading in the general direction he was going, he decided to thumb a lift. He shouted and waved his arms to attract attention as he ran towards the Holly Bush-Bentley road intent upon intercepting it, but suddenly the coach was just no longer there. It had completely vanished.

The Headless Horseman and Phantom Coach of Manifold Valley

A phantom white horse with a headless rider is said to gallop through the Manifold Valley on moonlit nights. It is alleged to be the ghost of a peddler, murdered by two men who cut off his head and set his headless body back on his horse.

There is also a coach which travels along the road to the ruined Throwley Hall. In the daytime, only the sound of its wheels can be heard, but at night its lights are seen. This particular coach has been given the name Cromwell Coach because of its connection to Robert Meverell of Throwley Hall, whose memorial is in Ilam Church. His daughter married Thomas, Lord Cromwell. It is said that this phantom coach and horses travels between Throwley Hall and turns round in the courtyard of Ilam Hall.

The Phantom Coach of Leam Hall, Eyam

Prior to 1939, when Leam Hall became part of the Youth Hostel Association, it was a private mansion of considerable charm. It reverted back to a private residence in the mid-1950s, although this story dates from the earlier period when admittance to the courtyard was through a pair of large white gates which were kept closed. This meant that they had to be opened and closed immediately before and after the entrance or exit of any person or vehicle.

The Cromwell Coach travels through this remote valley past the ruined Throwley Hall.

Above and right: *Phantom coaches are regularly seen on Peak District roads. Could it be the Peveril of the Peak, which is advertised on this old poster. (Courtesy of Buxton Museum)*

One evening, the groom and his boy assistant left the stables to meet what they believed to be the family carriage returning home. Both could hear the distinct sound of galloping horses and as the sound came nearer they waited at the entrance in readiness to open the gates for the coach bearing their returning master and mistress. But instead of the familiar carriage, a strange carriage and pair appeared round the bend of the drive, galloped towards them and disappeared through the closed white gates. The two men stared in shocked disbelief because the coachman had no head.

The Highwayman Who Lived a Double Life

The Woodlands is an isolated property on Darley Moor with a history of mysterious fires, which legend tells us can be traced back to centuries ago, when the site was occupied by a lonely wayside inn named the Quiet Woman. But the landlady was not quiet, she was surly and sullen and her unpleasant attitude discouraged customers who stopped for sustenance and shelter. Some tales tell that not only did she discourage them, but she made a habit of robbing and murdering them, and then buried their bodies in the cellar.

Understandably, business became so bad that the landlord had to find some other form of employment, and turned to highway robbery to supplement their income. Then one dark night, this robber/landlord was wounded by his intended victim, who broke free and headed for the supposed safety of the inn.

A few minutes later, his injured assailant arrived home and was pushed into the cellar to hide. In the scuffle that ensued, an oil lamp was knocked over and fire spread rapidly across the room, trapping the unfortunate man in the cellar. The landlady escaped the fire but the experience left her deranged. Another version said she was hanged for her crimes, but returned to re-enact the accident for eternity.

The vastly altered building became a farmhouse, then in 1966, a country club known as Moor Lane Sporting Club on the same site was gutted by fire. The owner confided to friends that he had experienced odd happenings and was especially concerned that his dog took fright for no apparent reason. He probably had reason to worry because during subsequent re-building, a caravan he occupied was also gutted by fire.

The property that occupies the site now gives little hint of its gruesome past.

four

Beasts, Bones and Odours

The Old House Museum, Bakewell

This intriguing old house is one of the oldest surviving domestic properties in the Peak. It was built as a parsonage house in the reign of Henry VIII and the first written record dates from 1534 when the Dean and Chapter of Lichfield handed the lease to Ralph Gell of Hopton, a local lawyer, sheep-farmer and lead dealer. In the late-sixteenth century it was extended to become a farmhouse, but by the eighteenth century it had been converted into five small tenements each with a staircase leading to a first-floor bedroom for Arkwright's mill workers. A sixth dwelling, now demolished, was built onto the south-east corner and four more families were accommodated by the conversion of the adjoining barn. The Arkwrights sold it to the Duke of Devonshire who sold it to the then master of the Bakewell workhouse, a Mr Cunningham and for many years the place was known as Cunningham Place. The last family to occupy the building was the Harrisons but over the years there had been very little attempt to stop the decay and in 1954 the house was condemned as unfit for human habitation.

The Old House Museum, where a number of unexplained incidents have been reported.

Just before the bulldozers moved in, it was saved by the newly formed Bakewell and District Historical Society who have restored and conserved the building we know today as the Old House Museum.

It is therefore not surprising that with such a long and chequered past there is some ghostly activity. Things in everyday use often go missing. One member of staff 'mislaid' an item of stationery she knew had been left on a shelf in her office. 'Would you mind returning that item were you found it?' she asked the empty room. Next morning it was back on the shelf.

The museum is ably manned by a dedicated group of volunteers. One of the ladies told me that she was upstairs sorting through some things when she heard the front door open and footsteps walking along the stone floor. This surprised her as she knew the door was locked and she was in the building on her own. Because of the gaps between the floor boards, it is possible to see through from the first floor down to the ground floor, and she peered through the cracks to see who could possibly have entered. She could see no one and the room appeared to be empty but, unconvinced, she called out. There was no reply. She went downstairs to check, but despite a thorough search, she was alone. Others will tell similar stories but all are in agreement that the spirits of the Old House Museum are not malign. Members of various paranormal groups have spent the night at the Old House Museum but despite elaborate procedures have found nothing specific. That is not to say that the place does not possess a resident spirit or two, it definitely does. A visit is certainly recommended, not just to enjoy a fascinating look at the various aspects of past social life in and around Bakewell but you may just experience more than you anticipate.

The Ghostly Duel at Youlgreave Hall

The skirmishes that took place between the Cavaliers and Roundheads during the Civil War have certainly left their mark, not only on our history but on our psychic landscape. Ghosts in the distinctive uniform of each side turn up quite regularly,

Occupants at Youlgreave Hall wait in trepidation for November when they are likely to be woken by the sound of ghostly swords clashing in one of the bedrooms. It is now referred to as the Duel Room as this is where two Civil War soldiers, a Cavalier and a Roundhead, are reputed to have fought to the death one dark November night back in the 1640s. The fight is said to be re-enacted on each anniversary.

Many years ago, technicians were called in to make a recording of this conflict. The clash of swords and the seventeenth-century cries and curses of the men would surely make great listening. Everything was set. The commentator sat waiting, the sound-recordists held their breath in anticipation and sure enough the sounds began to materialise in the best ghost-story tradition, then they ceased. The commentator dashed over to the where the sound-recordists crouched over their equipment. 'Did you hear it? Did you get it alright?' he asked excitedly.

'Cause I didn't,' snapped the engineer. 'You switched off the microphone.'

The commentator denied it and went to check. Not only had the microphone been switched off, the electricity had also been disconnected. They had checked and double checked before they left it and everyone present denied touching it, so what had happened. Who had stopped the recording?

Arkwright's Cromford Legacy

In 1769, a Lancashire barber and wig-maker had a bright idea for the mass production of yarn and cloth. What he needed was a reliable, constant and controllable source of water which he found at Cromford where he could harness the energy and the fast-flowing intensity of the River Derwent to drive the first successful, water-powered cotton mill.

Youlgreave Hall where a Cavalier and a Roundhead still re-enact their duel every November.

The labour force was originally drawn from the local farming and mining communities, but as production increased, workers were brought into the area and a whole new town was built to house them. Not only did Arkwright supply living accommodation, he also provided a school because he insisted that all children working at his mill must be able to read and write.

This was in sharp contrast to other mill owners who recruited pauper children and exploited child labour. Health and safety considerations were unknown factors. Workers toiled long hours and suffered hard and often sadistic measures, and although there was little documentation, it is known that the mortality rate was high, particularly amongst children. It is therefore not surprising to find that there are a lot of old mills that are haunted by these spectral children that are often referred to as radiants as they seem to exude a radiance or glow from their ghostly, almost transparent, diaphanous bodies. In contrast, the only reported incident of a ghost child at Arkwright's mill happened a few years ago when the old machine shop was being converted into the shop in the yard. A member of staff at the time took a photograph of the area but when it was processed, there was the image of a ghostly little girl on the print.

Many years ago, the second, larger mill on the site was totally destroyed by fire and now only the blackened end wall still remains. Apparently a ghostly Victorian policeman tries to raise the alarm by banging frantically on the outside door of the block, which now houses the exhibition centre. Many people have heard him, as recently as 1995, but one woman actually came face to face with him as she flung open the door; he was there for a second, and then disappeared.

People have reported a feeling of oppression in what is now the exhibition centre on the third floor of the first mill building. At one time, this was a laundry, but workers would not stay there alone.

Lights are known to switch on and off on their own, but the strangest thing occurred about four years ago when a guide was escorting a family group round the mill. They were taking a keen interest and eventually they arrived at the exhibition room where one of them asked the guide something about Arkwright. Before he could answer, the father, who later admitted to having psychic powers, said, 'Ask him yourself. He's standing right next to you!'

With houses, a chapel, shops, a school, a church and an impressive hotel, Cromford became a self-sufficient community and as such, it also needed a village lock-up. Used mainly for detaining drunks and nuisances, it was a rare occurrence when John Thompson was incarcerated there for four weeks after stealing a bale of cotton from Arkright's mill. Apparently this was not his first offence and after being declared guilty, he was sentenced to be transported to Australia. Whether he managed to avoid his sentence or whether he simply returned is unsure, but apparently John Thompson came back in body and in spirit. His ghost is said to haunt the lock-up where orbs and cold spots have been experienced by many visitors.

One hardy soul decided to raise money for charity by staying overnight in the lock-up, but he had to call it off in the middle of the night. Apparently he had been thoroughly spooked by the face of an old gaoler peering through the bars at him.

Richard Arkwright still haunts Cromford Mill.

Ilam Hall

The most breathtaking view of the picturesque village of Ilam is via the open, twisting road from Blore. A natural starting point for exploring the Manifold valley, Ilam, is where this remarkable river regains its overground course after its four-mile, subterranean journey through an underground lake.

A hall has stood at Ilam since John Port had the first one built in 1546, but in 1820, the estate was bought by Jesse Russell, who made a fortune as a soap manufacturer when washing was becoming fashionable. He gave the hall to his eldest son Jesse Russell jnr who married Mary Watts, sole heiress to David Pike Watts. When he died in 1816, Jesse and Mary took the additional name of Watts, and it is Mary who commissioned the magnificent memorial to her father, seen in Ilam Church.

Mary and Jesse Watts-Russell made Ilam their principle country home and radically changed its appearance by demolishing the old hall and building their new home in baronial splendour. Because the valley and surrounding hills reminded them of the Alps, they are also responsible for the Swiss look, which is such a feature of Ilam scenery. After producing eight children, Mary died at the early age of forty-eight and in her memory Jesse commissioned the gothic cross that stands in the centre of the village.

The Hall, still an imposing and stately structure, had a substantial part demolished when it was presented by Sir Robert McDougall to the National Trust to form a Youth Hostel in 1934. Now owned by the YHA it also has a resident ghost and visits from a phantom coach and horses which has been seen turning round in one of the old courtyards. Footsteps and noises have been heard around the stable block at night.

A lady in white is seen wandering through the corridors of the hall, through the Italian Garden and on to the church. Could this be Mary revisiting the home she loved?

Ilam Hall with the church, where the ghostly organist played, in the background.

A story told to me by a member of the National Trust staff involves a resident of Ilam who does not wish to be identified, so we will call him Joe. One evening, Joe left his comfortable fireside to lock the church. It was only a short distance from his home, but it was cold and dark and not the kind of night to loiter. Before locking the church door, he did a cursory check of the inside, sweeping his torch round the empty church, yet it was not empty. Sitting at the organ was a ghostly figure and ethereal music filled the church. Without stopping to investigate further, Joe turned and ran.

Throwley Hall

Throwley Hall is a sixteenth-century manor house nestling on a spur overlooking the Manifold Valley, on the southern boundary of Derbyshire between the villages of Ilam and Carlton. The hall's isolated position is relieved by Throwley Hall Farm, a Georgian-built working farm specialising in pedigree Charolais cattle, but the farm does not detract from the impressive ruins. Three hundred years ago, Throwley Hall was a great house, but the roof was removed around 1910 and the structure has been open to the wind and rain since.

On the western side of the house stood a chapel, the foundation stone bearing the initials F.M. A headless lady repeatedly appears from this chapel at midnight to terrify unsuspecting passers-by. One local lady not only confirmed this, she was convinced that the headless spectre followed her for a mile down the valley before going back. And if that isn't enough to prevent you wandering past Throwley Hall, there is also the spectre of the little boy lost. He is reported to be golden-haired and perfectly charming. He asks for directions home, but when asked where he lives, the boy points towards Throwley Hall, starts to sob then promptly disappears.

The Holloway Orphan

Writing over a century ago in his *Days of Derbyshire*, Dr Spencer T. Hall told the haunting tale of the Holloway couple, Philip and his first wife Martha, a cousin of Spencer Hall, who adopted a baby girl and brought her up as their own.

The child was still very young when one day she became very upset, saying that she could see a woman who wanted to embrace her. Because the woman could not be seen by anyone else, this could have been put down to the child's over active imagination, but when the child described her, the adoptive parents believed she could have been describing her natural mother who lived in Derby. The apparition stayed with the child following her to a neighbour's house, and then suddenly vanished in a flash of fire.

Several days later, news reached the family that the child's natural mother had been burnt to death but throughout her agonizing last minutes had begged to be taken to see her child one last time. The time coincided precisely with that when the apparition had appeared to the child.

The Whining Spectre

One winter day, a man from Fairfield, Buxton visited a farm three miles away. During his visit, there was a severe snowstorm and the man had to spend the night on the couch in the parlour. He was comfortable enough, yet he kept being disturbed by the loud whining of a dog in the room. Next morning, the guest told the farmer about the noisy dog, but the farmer declared that there was no dog. What he had heard was the spectre of their pet that had died three years previously.

There are other stories of ghost dogs that haunt particular places in the Peak District. At least one farm claims that the appearance of a ghost dog warns of bad weather. The dog is known to take it upon himself to round up the sheep on the hills in anticipation of the bad weather.

Another local tale tells of the customer that walked into the bar of a remote pub. He looked around and noticed a dog lying by the welcoming coal fire. The man purchased his drink and was about to walk over to warm himself by the fire but first he thought he should check whether the dog was friendly towards strangers.

'Is the dog going to object to me sharing his hearth?' the man asked the barman.

'What dog?' replied the barman.

The man turned to the fire but there was no sign of the dog. He tried to explain to the barman who smiled knowingly.

'That's a sure sign,' he said. 'That dog and his master died in a snow storm while trying to round up the sheep and now it always appears to warn others that bad weather is on the way.'

Was The House Haunted?

Kath and Dennis Dell were enthusiastic about re-vamping the old house they had just bought until Kath sensed a strange atmosphere and began to suspect the place was haunted. When one weekend they had friends to stay, they brought their pet dog Randal, who rushed around the house sniffing excitedly until he reached the stairs. There he stopped in his tracks, his tail between his legs. He then let out a deep growl, turned and ran into the kitchen. After that they couldn't get him any further.

Kath had heard that dogs and cats can sense ghosts, so she decided to experiment and asked another friend if she would bring her cat round. The cat was allowed to roam freely and he meandered round the house quite happily. He even bounded up the stairs, with his mistress and Kath following, but as soon as he entered the main bedroom, he stopped. His back arched, his fur fluffed up and he hissed at something in the corner of the room.

This completely unnerved Kath. She was now sure that her earlier instinct was correct and both animals had seen or sensed something paranormal. Dennis was unconvinced, but he did agree to ask the neighbours if they could borrow their dog and he told them why. The neighbours listened with interest then told them that an old man had died in the house some time ago and other people living there had also felt his presence. Once Kath had had her gut-feeling confirmed, she arranged for an exorcism, they got on with the re-vamp and lived there happily for many years.

Bella Could Detect the Spirit in the Room

It was the end of September. Barbara Oakley and her friend Barbara Dunks decided to take a short holiday at the Peak District town of Castleton, with their dogs Bella, a Cavalier King Charles Spaniel, and Mr Ching, a Pekingese. Unfortunately, the short holiday was even shorter than anticipated.

Everything was fine until they were shown into their room at a B&B establishment on the outskirts of the town and Bella began acting as if she was in great discomfort. Thinking she might want to relieve herself, Barbara took her out for a walk. Once outside, she was back to being her usual happy, boisterous self, but as soon as they returned to their room, Bella started acting strangely again.

They prepared to go to bed, thinking that perhaps then Bella would curl up in her basket and go to sleep, yet despite having her own familiar bedding, Bella just wouldn't settle. She paced the floor, her breathing became heavy and erratic; she was very jumpy and kept looking round anxiously. Barbara was at a loss what to do.

Mr Ching, who until then had been unfazed by everything, went to Bella as if to see what the problem was, then he tried to hide under the bed. When that wasn't successful he shot into the bathroom and spent the night there. Throughout the night Bella paced round the room refusing to settle. Her laboured breathing was painfully difficult as if she was fighting for oxygen and Barbara was so worried, she telephoned her vet thirty miles away and got an early morning appointment.

The night hours stretched endlessly and at first light they set off back home, but almost before they had left Castleton, Bella was fast asleep in the back of the car breathing perfectly evenly and showing no signs of agitation. The vet could find no reason for the problem and it has never re-occurred. He said it was possible that something had disturbed her, but what? Did Bella suffer a panic attack caused by something only she could see or sense in that room?

The Dog and the Cottage at Longnor

After Mr Wood had experienced several strange phenomena at his Longnor home, he enlisted the help of a medium. She confirmed that there was a supernatural presence in the house which had some connection with an old man and a dog. The medium also thought that there could be a body buried under the cottage. The medium's words were not discounted as poppycock because during the seventeenth century there was a shroud tax levied on burials in public churchyards, and to avoid this, house-burials were in practise in many areas. It was also believed that no building would be secure unless a living creature was incorporated into the foundations, a rather barbaric tradition that was practiced in both religious and secular buildings.

Mr Wood was able to confirm that the sound of a growling dog could often be heard coming from the fireplace, then one day it was necessary to relay a wobbly flag-stone in the floor. As he prised the flagstone up and began to shovel earth from beneath it, a horrific shape like a large dog emerged from the ground, leapt away and disappeared.

Dicky's Skull – The Cranial Guardian of Tunstead Farm

In 1996 Andy Roberts and David Clarke completed a comprehensive study on the theory that human skulls kept in old houses must never be taken away or bad luck, illness or even death will follow. They identified twenty-seven known examples throughout the British Isles, the most famous of which was that of Dicky at Tunstead Farm in the Peak District. Its exploits have been told in prose and at least two poems, and at one time it was so famous visitors could buy postcards with the photograph of Dicky on his favourite window sill at Tunstead Farm.

Tenants who treated the skull with respect found it a talisman against evil and hardship, but when it was discarded, cattle strayed or died, crops failed, and accidents happened. It was thrown into Comb's reservoir and the fish died. Twice when it was buried in the churchyard, misfortunes multiplied. While the farmhouse was being revamped, the skull was thrown into a manure heap and the workmen were persistently hindered until it was returned to a more dignified position. Many calamities could be credited to human error, yet the frequency and regularity of bad-luck and misfortunes that happened when Dicky was disturbed were more than just coincidental.

The most outstanding achievement accredited to Dicky was 'his' victory over the London & North Western Railway Co. In order to carry their line north, they needed to cross one of Tunstead Farm's fields, which necessitated building a bridge and embankment. Despite many attempts, foundations sank, sections of the bridge collapsed, workmen fell ill, and rumours that the project was jinxed did little to help the situation. Local residents said it was Dicky who objected to the building work, and eventually, the railway company and contractors gave up battling with the malign power and sited an alternative route. This led the dialect poet, Samuel Laycock to write:

> Neaw Dickey, be quiet wi' thee lad
> An' let navvies an' railway be.
> Mon, tha shouldn't do soa, it's too bad,
> What harm are they doin' to thee?
> Deed folk shouldn't meddle at o'
> But leov o' these matters to th' wick.
> They'll see they're done gradely, aw know –
> Dos't y'ear what aw say to thee, Dick?

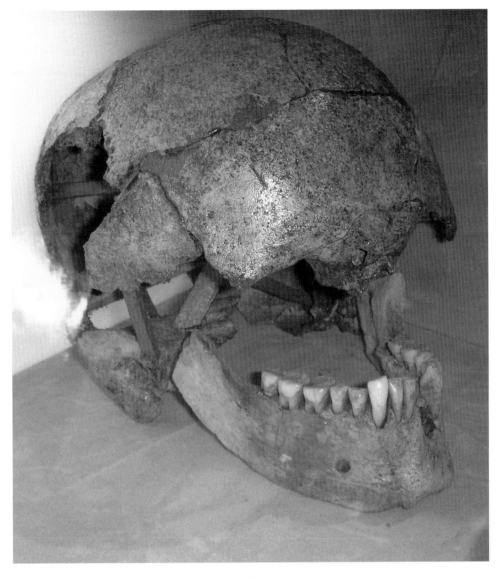

Skulls were often kept as good luck talismans. (Courtesy of Buxton Museum)

The word 'wick' is often thought to mean weak, but a true Derbyshire native knows that this means that he/she is quick witted, as in the well-known rhyme:

> Derbyshire born and Derbyshire bred
> Strong i' the arm and wick i' the 'ead.

Some say this cranial guardian was a soldier named Ned Dickinson who returned from the Huguenot Wars in France to claim his land, but found that his cousin Jack

Johnson had taken possession in the belief that Ned was dead. He soon was! The treacherous cousin and his wife are said to have chopped off his head and buried him in the garden, but one winter night, the gruesome head materialised in the farmhouse where it has remained ever since.

Another story says that the skull was that of one of two heiresses who was murdered for her share of the inheritance. After this, the farmhouse was haunted by frightful noises which intensified until they were unbearable. Somehow this was linked to the murder victim who was dug up. Her head was placed on the windowsill and peace returned, so there it remained. The skull was scientifically tested and found to be female, so perhaps Ned Dickinson was in fact Nedetia Dickinson.

A skull was kept on a window sill at Dunscar Farm near Castleton, and another at Flagg Hall, south of Buxton. Again tradition warns that the skull's removal or abuse will foretell misfortune. At Flagg Hall, south of Buxton, an attempt was made to bury the skull in the nearby Chelmorton churchyard, but when the horses drawing the improvised hearse reached a point known as Chelmorton Thorn, they refused to go any further. They stamped and reared as though confronted by some invisible force and the driver had no choice but to turn round and return the recalcitrant skull to the Hall.

Skulls are popularly associated with witchcraft and divination and a medium for communication with the world of the spirits, but Mrs Lomas, a former resident of Flagg Hall said the skull was part of a human skeleton which was the professional property of a surgeon who once lived there. Such skeletons were often stolen from graveyards by 'resurrectionists,' better known as 'body snatchers' who disposed of them to members of the medical profession for experimental purposes.

Curzon Lodge, Brassington

This article is taken from the *Derbyshire Advertiser* of 31 October 1913, showing that 100 years ago, our ancestors were interested in the paranormal exactly as we are today.

Running through the wild bleak environs of Brassington and Longcliffe, between Longcliffe and Grangemill, Curzon Lodge seems an oasis in the midst of stormy, desolate wilds. From here is an excellent view of Harbour Rocks, a possible Druidic circle. Mr Isaac Rains who resides at Curzon Lodge knows the antiquarian lore of the area better than most. A few years ago, two barrows or lows were opened and in one was found a cist containing skulls and bones. A skull from the Longcliffe cave is preserved by Mr Rains.

In the opinion of Mr Rains, the farm was originally part of the land belonging to a monastery at Aldwark, an off-shoot from that of Darley, passing to the Curzon's of Kedleston Hall in the reign of Henry VIII.

The house is also haunted. His niece and a serving girl have actually seen the apparition, that of a young girl who comes and stands for a moment on the doorstep.

And surely this lonely ancient farmhouse is a fitting milieu for the manifestations of the unseen, for without being superstitious or credulous it is illogical for us to deny the possibility if not the probability of occasional visible tokens of its presence.

Right: So many farmers were keeping historical finds as souvenirs the authorities issued a poster to try to locate ancient artefacts.

Below: Farmers were asked to keep a lookout for ancient artefacts.

Above Illustrations are reduced in size

Notice to Farmers and others.

It is desirable to preserve all Flint or Bronze Implements found in the soil by placing them in the Museum at the Town Hall, Buxton. The above sketches will indicate the kind of objects that are usually found. Any farmer or others who discover such objects are requested to kindly report the same to the Curator of the Museum, Town Hall, Buxton. The Committee will pay a fair value if the finder is disposed to sell.

BY ORDER.

Clog Hall

The isolation of many houses and High Peak farms has helped to keep native traditions alive, so it is not surprising to find that many still rely upon traditional charms and a good deal of superstition to protect their homes. Although some talisman, like the skulls, are not to modern taste, items like horseshoes, and old boots and shoes are more popular. From at least the sixteenth century, a standard way of wishing someone good luck on a journey, or success in a new undertaking, was to throw an old shoe after them. From the 1820s, shoe-throwing was increasingly popular as a wedding custom and it became an acceptable practise to fling a shoe after a newly-married couple. It was probably a combination of direct hits and the increased used of wedding carriages that changed the custom. Today people no longer throw shoes, but it is quite common to attach them to the wedding car.

With a history as good-luck charms, it is not surprisong therefore to find items of footwear concealed down old mines and in the foundations of buildings. A pair of clogs was once preserved at Thorneylea Farm near Chapel-en-le-Frith, with a warning against moving them for fear of the dire consequences that may result.

They were such a conversation piece that the farm became known as Clog Hall even after one stout-hearted resident decided enough was enough and threw the clogs into the fire.

Dozens of these talisman were once used and feared in the High Peak, so it is likely that many lie forgotten under floors or staircases or even in the walls or foundations, where they will continue to do what they were originally intended to do – protect the homes of those who live there.

Old shoes were good luck talismans.

The Missing Red Shoes

It was New Year's Day 1815 and at the Wardlow Mires toll house at the junction of the roads from Stoney Middleton and Bakewell, a large, impatient crowd was gathering. They were anxious to pay their dues and pass but there was no sign of Mrs Hannah Oliver the toll keeper. It seemed highly unlikely that she would desert her post, but the noise of stamping horses, men shouting and blasts on a bugle brought the barmaid from the nearby inn to see what was happening. Going in search of Hannah, she was horrified to find her lifeless body hanging over the doorstep. At first it was thought that Hannah had taken her own life, but it was soon obvious that she had been strangled with a handkerchief. Hannah had been murdered.

The police were soon on the scene. They carried out a thorough examination and interviewed everyone close by. Money had been stolen, but the odd thing about the case was that Hannah had no shoes on her feet and there were no shoes nearby. What made this so strange was that only a short time before she'd had a pair of red shoes made especially for her by the local shoe-maker Mr Samuel Marsden of Stoney Middleton. She had been so thrilled with her new shoes that she had worn them constantly, yet there was now no trace of them.

The shoes had actually been taken by twenty-one-year-old Anthony Lingard of Tideswell who had earlier murdered Hannah. He gave the shoes and the money to his girlfriend who was pregnant with his child in the hope that she would father the child on another man. She asked where he had obtained the money and the shoes which she suspected were stolen and, because he couldn't give an acceptable answer, she refused to accept them. Lingard then tried to hide them in a hay-stack, but a few days later he removed them and took them home. It was around this time that the suspicious manner in which Lingard was acting began to attract attention and the police were alerted. They searched his room and found the pair of shoes, but they alone gave insufficient evidence to convict him.

The police however, took the shoes to Samuel Marsden the shoe maker who recognised the shoes immediately and proceeded to strip one down. He knew that if they were Hannah's shoes inside he had incorporated a piece of packing on which was written 'Commit no Crime.' When this was found, Lingard's fate was sealed.

The trial was held in Derby and the verdict was that Lingard should be hanged, and then gibbeted at the scene of the crime as an example to all, so Anthony Lingard was hanged at Derby on 8 March 1815.

His body was conveyed to Wardlow but on reaching Rowsley, the escort proceeded on through Beeley instead of continuing on the main road to Bakewell. Soon they entered the private grounds of Chatsworth House where they were met by a servant of the Duke of Devonshire who ordered them to halt by order of the duke.

'Duke he may be,' replied the officer in charge, 'but I have the King's Commission. We will proceed.' The grim procession continued on its way and from that day forth, the road was no longer considered private under an ancient law that specified that the passage of a corpse along a road made the road a public right of way.

Arriving at Wardlow, tradesmen had already set up stalls catering for the huge crowds who flocked to see the gruesome spectacle, and a Methodist minister named Longdon even addressed the crowds from under the very gibbet using the shocking sight to emphasise the message of his sermon

The cost of apprehending Lingard was £31 5s 5d; the cost of the gibbeting was £53 18s 8d plus 10 guineas for the gaoler who conveyed the body from Derby to Wardlow. Lingards body hung in the gibbet for several months and the new toll-keepers were constantly reminded of the gruesome crime by the sound of the skeleton rattling in its frame. When it was finally taken down the skull was sent to Belle Vue where it was put on display, but the grisly crime has left a ghostly legacy. Cyclists riding through Wardlow Mires have reported the touch of invisible hands and the peculiar, sickening feeling of being strangled, so is Lingard's ghost still enacting that dreadful deed?

Digging up the Past

Overton Hall and grounds of approximately 1,000 acres originally belonged to the Overton family. The estate was handed to the Hunts in 1327, then in 1599 purchased by William Hodgkinson of Northedge. This thirty-roomed lumpish mansion passed by marriage to the Banks family and so to Sir Joseph Banks, the distinguished naturalist.

At the age of eighteen, Joseph Banks came into a considerable inheritance enabling him to pursue his keen interest in botany in adventurous style. In 1766 he undertook the first of his discovery voyages to Newfoundland, was made a Fellow of the Royal Society, then from 1768-71 accompanied Captain James Cook aboard HMS *Endeavour*, acting as the supervisory scientist on the Royal Society's famed expedition to the South Seas. They returned with a vast collection of botanical specimens, and Sir Joseph planted a wide variety of rare trees and shrubs in the parklands and grounds of Overton Hall. It became known for its horticulture, but there were other things more sinister than plants buried there.

In 1884 when digging the foundations for a wall, seven skeletons were unearthed. All were big, heavy men with their skulls broken. They were re-interred in Ashover churchyard but nothing was discovered to throw any light on the reason for the rather unorthodox burial in the grounds at Overton. Some reports say they appeared to have been buried hastily, perhaps as a result of plague but that would not account for their damaged skulls.

Sir Joseph died on 19 June 1820 without issue and the property passed to Dr John Bright, and then the Jessop family. In the 1930s it was let to the Youth Hostel Association, was a boarding school for boys evacuated from Derby school during the first part of the Second World War, then an approved school followed by a residential home for the elderly. In 1956, a story was reported in the press that the wife of a Pentecostal pastor living at Overton Hall had left because it was haunted. The figure of a woman, thought to be the third wife of one of the Jessops is said to haunt the forecourt. Perhaps she doesn't approve of the way the property has fared over the years but as it is now converted into residential apartments, she may be able to rest in peace at last.

The Last Live Gibbet in Derbyshire

One day, a tramp called at a thatched cottage in Baslow begging for food, and although she was cooking bacon for herself at the time, the lady of the house told him she had no food for lazy ruffians like him. This so incensed the tramp that he forced his way inside, grabbed the pan and poured the boiling fat down her throat, scalding her to death.

Following his arrest and trial, he was sentenced to be hung in chains from a gibbet erected on Gibbet Moor just off the main Baslow/Chesterfield road, to die a slow and painful death. Well-meaning people brought him food but that just prolonged his agony. His screams were said to have so upset the Duke of Devonshire at Chatsworth House directly west of Gibbet Moor, that he brought about the legislation to prohibit such an inhuman practice.

Above and below: *Seven skeletons were dug up at Overton Hall. (Courtesy of Buxton Museum)*

This unknown tramp was the last person in England to be gibbeted alive and the man's screams are still heard. In July 1992 Jane Townsend reported hearing what she described as bloodcurdling and petrifying screams while hiking in the area of Gibbet Moor.

But this is a double haunting. The cottage at Baslow is also said to be haunted by the murdered woman. According to the late Edgar Osbourne, a retired librarian and archivist at Chatsworth House who lived in the cottage, during times of illness when he was in much pain, the old woman appeared at his bedside and soothed him.

Ordeal by Touch

Almost two centuries ago, a woman sent her maidservant to collect water from the well, but the girl took so long that when she returned, the woman thrashed her unmercifully. The poor girl died from her injuries and although the woman was brought to trial, she called upon an old law that declared that 'should the murderer touch his victim, the wounds would bleed anew.' This was known as Ordeal by Touch, and because the wounds did not suddenly spurt blood when the woman touched them, she was considered innocent and set free.

She may have escaped the gallows, but her ordeal was about to begin because from then on, every night she was visited by the ghost of the deceased maid who always stayed until cock-crow. These visits so terrified the woman that she paid people to stay with her overnight and often, fortified by alcohol, these individuals caused such a disturbance, fights broke out amongst the inebriated visitors.

Eventually a gathering of clergy was summoned to exorcise the ghost, but it would not go quietly. In the end the spirit was finally put to rest on the hills where, from then on, it appeared as a dim light. Locals recognised it as the phantom, and coachmen pointed it out to their passengers and acquainted them with the story of the melancholic maid.

The Ghosts of Eyam

Eyam is tragically famous as the 'Derbyshire Plague Village', owing to the terrible events which began in September 1665 when the deadly infection was brought to the village in a box of cloth from London. The cloth was for a journeyman tailor named George Vicars who lodged in a cottage by the church, with Mary Cooper, a widow with two small children. The cloth was damp so George spread it out in front of the fire to dry, but within a few days he was ill and died an agonising death. Within a fortnight one of the children was also dead, four more deaths occurred before the end of September and as more deaths followed, the dreadful fact became clear: Eyam had been struck by the deadly plague.

The whole village was in a state of panic. Wealthy residents and those who had somewhere to go left in a hurry, but most of the villagers had no alternative but to stay in Eyam. Emergency measures were taken to isolate them from their neighbouring towns and villages, food and rations were left at the boundary stones in exchange for money dropped into vinegar in the belief this would disinfect it. The church and churchyard were closed, and the dead were buried in the fields in hastily constructed graves.

Church services were conducted by the rector, Revd William Mompesson, who preached to his slowly diminishing congregation from a lofty rock in a dell called Cutlet's Delph. Gardens and farmland were neglected and overgrown; every house had become a mortuary and every remaining resident a mourner. The few inhabitants left had no heart for anything but marking the graves with stones to identify where their dear ones lay, then in November 1666, after a very long fifteen months, it was all over but 260 residents of Eyam were dead.

With such a sad history, it is hardly surprising that the village of Eyam is literally teaming with ghosts and stories of the paranormal. (Other stories appear in the author's books *Romantic Haunts of Derbyshire* and *Haunted Derbyshire*.)

When the present owners of the tea rooms in the heart of Eyam were recently revamping the place, they obviously disturbed many spirits. Drawers opened and closed, things went missing, and music turned on and off, but possibly the most bizarre thing was the door opening and closing and a voice calling, 'It's only me.' When anyone went to investigate they found no one there.

On the main road outside the tea rooms, many people have seen the ghost of a beautiful young girl who walks up and down the road. A white lady haunts further up the road, and across from the school, people often get the feeling of being choked.

Across the road from the churchyard is the Institute where people sense they are being watched and a cleaner saw the stage curtains moving as if someone was punching them from behind. She knew this wasn't possible as she was the only one in the building, and this so freaked her, she never worked late again.

The main street at Eyam in the 1920s.

The 'Plague Window' in Eyam Church.

At the side of the church, in the 'plague cottage' where it all began, the front bedroom is said to be haunted by a pleasant-faced lady in a blue smock. A former resident refused to sleep there after having his sleep disturbed so often. He would wake to find her watching him before simply fading away.

In the front churchyard is the grave of Catherine Mompesson, the rector's wife who died in August 1666. Her ghost is said to drift through the churchyard and pause near the Saxon cross. The whisper of her ghostly gown is said to be heard at Eyam Rectory where she died. In more recent times, it is not unusual for overnight guests to enquire next morning about who was ill in the night. They hear footsteps rushing along the corridor, doors opening and closing and the rustle of feminine dresses. A former maid at the rectory met a ghostly lady ascending the back stairs and afterwards when describing her, it was believed to be the ghost of Mrs Mompesson. The back churchyard is the haunt of many troubled souls including a young girl who skips around the gravestones in broad daylight and has been known to integrate with visiting children.

Further up the road, opposite the green, is Eyam Hall, where a young woman is reported to haunt a top-floor bedroom. Dogs will not go into that room and often people in the street have seen her looking out of the third window from the left. Eyam Hall once had a ghost in its garrets. It was that of an old man who was always seen sitting at a circular table in one of the top-storey rooms. The room was always kept locked by the owners of the hall.

The courtyard of the hall is closed by a solid gate but on one particular ghost walk, as seventeen people stood in the courtyard watching, the gate slowly closed, yet there had been no wind and no one near. The old laundry, which is accessed through the courtyard, is actually built over a well which, disregarding the grid, is still open in the centre of the room. Apparently many years ago, when repairing the sides of the well, they discovered human bones and, not knowing what to do with them, replaced them; ever since there have been strange sensations in that room. It can be either very cold or very warm for no apparent reason, and people have felt like passing out. Personally, I felt a tightening in my chest and throat, as if coming down with a cold. I had difficulty breathing due to the hot, damp atmosphere like you would experience in a sauna, but this was cloggy and stale, the soiled, dusty smell of dirty, wet clothes, soapy washing water and clothes being boiled.

The story dubbed 'the Village Spectre' first appeared in William Wood's book *The Tales and Traditions of the Peak* and dates from 1770. The Weldon family lived at a house on the south-eastern edge of Eyam, but the story is actually about Mary Weldon, the daughter of the house, who went to stay with friends in Lancashire. While there, she met and fell in love with young man named Baldwin Laycock. The affection was mutual and on the day before Mary left Lancashire, Baldwin asked her to marry him. Mary accepted and in high spirits Baldwin rode over to Eyam to ask Mary's father for her hand in marriage. The agreement was obviously acceptable and that evening as they waited for Mary to arrive back in Eyam, Baldwin sat with her father in the shade of the sycamore tree in the garden. After some time, they were on the point of retiring to the house when they were startled by the appearance of a shadowy form. It had a striking but deadly and cadaverous expression, yet there was a calmness on the silent face and a smile loitered on the colourless lips. Then the figure slowly dissolved, leaving Mr Weldon in a state of shocked disbelief.

When this disquieting experience was related to Mrs Weldon, she shared her husbands concern, and explained to the bewildered visitor that they had seen the village spectre. The ghost had been that of Isabel, the eighteen-year-old daughter of Squire Bradshaw of Bradshaw Hall. Isabel had been compelled to repudiate the affections of her true love and marry a suitor chosen by her father. About an hour after the forced wedding ceremony, the reluctant bride received news that her despairing lover had taken his own life, and a few hours later Isabel also breathed her last. Ever since that day, the spirit of Isabel appeared to forewarn of the death of anyone 'whose heart the tender passion fills' or to put it in modern-day parlance, it looked as though the love affair of Baldwin and Mary was about to come to an abrupt end.

As Baldwin Laycock and the Weldons waited anxiously, a messenger arrived with the news. The coach in which Mary Weldon was travelling home had been about ten miles from Eyam when it stopped. Mary stepped out, missed the step and fell under the vehicle, which passed over her body, causing fatal injuries. The time of the accident coincided with the appearance of the village spectre.

Bagshaw Hall

The road off North Church Street, Bakewell, directly opposite the turning to the museum is Bagshaw Hill. It is extremely steep and only part is accessible by car, but perched half way down the hill is Bagshaw Hall. It is possible that this was built on the site of Moor Hall, the manor of which was granted to Ralph Gernon by King John around the beginning of the thirteenth century. In 1209, Moor Hall was in the occupation of Geoffrey, second son of Sir William Gernon, and served for many centuries as a farmhouse. In 1502, the Moor Hall estate was bought by Sir Henry Vernon of Haddon and passed through marriage to the Manners and the Dukes of Rutland.

It was assumed that Moor Hall was demolished, but if Bagshaw Hall was built on the site of Moor Hall, which ceased to exist around the end of the seventeenth century, parts of Moor Hall, which would date from the early sixteenth century and possibly earlier, could have been incorporated into Bagshaw Hall.

The first reference to Bagshaw Hall was in 1648. It was understood that at this time a previous building on the site was enlarged and the fine Carolean façade added. This is credited to Thomas Bagshaw who gave the Hall his name. It was his pride and joy and to show off his new hall he invited all the local dignitaries to a feast so that they could admire his new abode. Amongst those that attended was the Duke of Rutland who enjoyed the hospitality of the house, then reminded the host that as the land on which the house was built was actually part of the Rutland estate, by rights he could legally take possession of any building on his land. If the duke could still claim ownership of the earlier Moor Hall incorporated into the building, he might have had a strong claim and with friends in high places, anything was possible. The comment may have been made in jest but Thomas Bagshaw was taking it very seriously. According to legend, Bagshaw was so distraught at the thought of loosing his beautiful hall that he apparently went into the attic, threw a rope over the beam and hanged himself. Ever since his ghost is said to wander the attic.

Bagshaw Hall.

Over the years, the property has been a private residence, the Conservative Club, an office complex and now is in the process of being converted into luxury residential and holiday lets. When it was an office complex, a courier making a delivery couldn't get out quickly enough after sensing the ghost. Recently one lady who lived there as a child admitted that they never played in the attic because of the strange feeling up there.

When one owner threw a party, in order to accommodate all his guests overnight, he and his wife planned to sleep in the attic. He was moving bedding up the stairs when he saw the ghostly figure of a man. Naturally this rather unnerved him but he decided to pass it off as an illusion and didn't mention it to his wife. That night she woke up screaming after feeling the sudden heavy weight of something on her legs and there on the bed sat a ghostly man. She shot down the stairs, leaving her husband to collect up the bedding, and they moved permanently out of the attic.

The Mystery of Moorseats

One Peak Land legend says that the powerful, land-owning Eyre clan had seven houses built on seven hills around the Hathersage valley. Each house could be seen from the other and the family used a form of semaphore to communicate to each other.

The stories of the paranormal activity of two of these houses – Highlow Hall and North Lees Hall – are told in *Romantic Haunts of Derbyshire*, but another of the halls that has a haunting presence is Moorseats, built on the hillside by St Michael's Church, Hathersage. It stands in a beautiful setting, and the present house, which dates from the seventeenth century, although much altered since, has all the characteristics of a small, Peak District gabled manor house.

When Charlotte Brontë stayed at Hathersage vicarage with her friend Elen Nussey during the summer of 1845, she drew her inspiration for one of her best-loved stories,

Jane Eyre, from the neighbourhood. She was particularly strongly influenced by two of the Eyre homes – North Lees Hall, which she called Thornfield, and Moorseats, which became Moor House, where her heroine Jane Eyre sheltered from a snow storm.

Could she have been influenced by the tales of the white lady who is said to haunt the house and ground of Moorseats? At dusk this ghostly figure has been seen to walk through an avenue of yew trees to a small-walled garden, previously an old orchard. What makes this phantom so unusual is the fact that she seems able to appear in the form of the current owners of the house and even relatively recently, the owner saw a white figure that he mistook for his six-year-old daughter flitting across the grass near the pond. It took him a few seconds to realise that his daughter could not possibly be there as she was actually at school.

Anyone sleeping in one particular bedroom is likely to be woken in the night by someone enquiring how they are feeling and one member of the family actually believed it to be her mother. Having had her sleep disturbed on so many occasions, and finding the ghostly intruder was not her mother, she reprimanded it so severely that it never disturbed her again.

In his 1973 book *Ghosts of Derbyshire*, Clarence Daniel told of the experience recounted to him by Brian Hickinson when he worked as a painter and decorator in an upstairs corridor at Moorseats. At the time, he was graining some woodwork and had left some brushes and a paint kettle while he went downstairs to the kitchen for a cup of tea. When he returned some time later, he found they had completely vanished. Initially he assumed this was some practical joke played by the occupiers, the Misses Hodgkinsons, yet they categorically denied it. No one else had been present in the house and as the brushes and paint kettle were never seen again, this remains one of the mysteries of Moorseats.

Castle Hill House, Bakewell

The elegant Castle Hill House was built in 1785 for Alexander Bossley, a Bakewell attorney and son of a Bakewell mercer. The house is a dignified Georgian construction and sits on the slope of Castle Hill, the name of which would imply that this is the site of the burgh or fortress, erected against the Danes by Edward the Elder in AD 924.

Alexander Bossley died unmarried in 1826 and the house passed to his cousin John Barker, a Sheffield lead merchant. He rented it out for a period before selling to the Duke of Rutland who used it initially as the residence of his agent. From then on the house had a continuous run of tenants, until in the post-war period, it became a country club, before being sold to the County Council for use as part of Lady Manner's School.

At some time in its chequered past, a rather tragic incident occurred and this incident has left paranormal activity in its wake. A butler named Jim Marlowe was finding life unbearable and one day he flipped. He left the butler's pantry closing the door behind him, walked along the corridor and up a flight of stairs to the gun-room where he selected a suitable gun then returned to the pantry where he locked the door behind him. A few minutes later, there was a loud bang and Jim Marlowe had shot himself.

Castle Hill House.

This sad incident happened on a Friday evening and apparently every Friday evening since, if you listen carefully you will hear Jim Marlowe re-creating his last walk from the pantry to the gun-room. There is a loose floor board at the entrance to this room and it is heard to creak ominously under the weight of the phantom's footstep.

Smelly Spirits

We began *Haunted Peak District* with a number of stories concerning sounds, so because spirits can activate all our senses, it might be fitting to end with a few stories concerning smell. Like all other mysterious psychic phenomena, how it happens is a complete mystery to which we can apply no logical explanation. All that we know is that the departed are somehow able to activate our sense of smell as a means of communicating with us.

New people moving into premises often detect strange smells, which can range from the stimulating scent of herbs and flowers to the less agreeable stench of blocked drains. I've known people actually call in pest controllers to locate certain disagreeable smells believing them to be decomposing vermin, yet these abstract odours usually appear to be without a visible cause. That leaves us with the knowledge that we are probably dealing with the paranormal and the mysterious fact that we are able to detect astral aromas or smelly spirits that appear to be able to briefly assail our nostrils. They can be pleasant or pungent, and usually have some deep meaning and association with the deceased.

Prior to the death of her mother, Mrs Nora Fullwood told how a combination of eucalyptus and disinfectant had been used for sanitary purposes and over a period of time, this particular pungent combination made Mrs Fullwood feel quite nauseous. After her mother's death, she was sitting quietly at home when she had a sudden strong feeling that her mother was in the room with her. In fact she felt that her mother was so close, if she reached out she could actually touch her. Instinctively she said 'Hello mother!' and at that moment the room was filled with an overwhelming smell of eucalyptus and disinfectant.

Another lady told how her father had been passionately fond of lilies of the valley, which flower in late spring, yet when he died in mid-January, the room was filled with the scent of lilies of the valley.

In a 1951 article in the *Derbyshire Countryside*, Geraldine Mellor recounted a tale concerning Yhelt Cottage, a sixteenth-century house near Buxton. During the period 1951-1953, the occupants were plagued by such poltergeist activity as crockery being rattled on the shelves, a hanging brass warming pan being swung like a pendulum, articles moving and electrics malfunctioning. Curious rosy lights appeared and disappeared on the bedroom walls and a strange, exquisite perfume-like incense always appeared to accompany these activities. A priest was brought in to apply the ritual of exorcism and the activity ceased, but he was also able to supply the knowledge that Yhelt Cottage had once been the site of a nunnery. It is highly probable that the fragrant odour was created by the various aromatic substances burnt for their fragrant odour in religious ceremonies performed at the nunnery.

The Smell of Sulphur at Stoney Middleton Hall

Stoney Middleton Hall is a former vicarage which the first Lord Denman had converted into his summer residence. Lord Denman was Lord Chief Justice in 1832 and Baron Denman of Dovedale in 1834. He was one of the ablest of Whig lawyer politicians at the time of the Reform Bill and played a prominent part in the suppression of slavery.

There is no record of any ghosts at Stoney Middleton Hall but there are a number of instances of phantom fragrances. People sleeping in a certain bedroom are affected by the strange, inexplicable smell of sulphur, yet there is no fire in or anywhere near the room. It was so strong and insufferable on one occasion when the daughter of the house and a friend slept in this room that not only did it wake them, they had to get up and open the window.

A much more pleasant aroma drifted into the dreams of some friends who were staying with the Jessops at the time when they owned the house. They were woken by the appetizing aroma of bacon frying, yet in the small hours of the night it wasn't a midnight snack or an early breakfast. Not only was no meal of any sort being cooked, the bedroom was so far from the kitchen, they were unlikely to have smelt anything if it was.

Smoking Ban

One of the most common spiritual experiences at old inns is the smell of tobacco smoke. Guests and staff at the Rutland Arms, Bakewell, regularly report this, but it's also quite common in private houses.

Gordon and Hannah Robinson are non-smokers and when friends and neighbours visit they respect their wishes not to smoke in their Eyam home, but how can you stop a ghost from leaving the smell of tobacco all around the house?

'We never actually see the smoke or the ghost,' said Gordon, 'but the smell is unmistakable. We don't mind having a ghost. He isn't any trouble and we would hardly notice him if it wasn't for the pipe smoking.'

A couple from Bonsal had a slightly different experience. They could not only smell the unmistakable smell of cigar smoke they could also see the wisps of blue smoke as it curled upwards from a cigar. What made this even spookier was the fact that there was never any sign of a cigar or the smoker.

The Pipe-Smoking Ghost of Goss Hall

Goss Hall or Gorse Hall as it was formerly known, dates back to the sixteenth century and stands above the village of Ashover on the coach road to Overton Hall. It was originally owned by the Deincourt family and eventually passed to a member of the Babbington family. Anthony Babbington is said to have taken refuge in the cellar of Goss Hall following the discovery of his plot to rescue Mary Stuart, Queen of Scots, from Wingfield Manor.

The Hall is also said to have belonged to Sir Walter Raleigh for a short time prior to this, so is it surprising that it should have a ghost that smokes a pipe which fills the house with tobacco smoke? (Sir Walter introduced tobacco to this country.)

The smell was apparently so bad in the 1950s that is caused one owner to leave, and although it became almost a ruin, Goss Hall is now a very desirable private house.

A Fusty Phantom

There are a number of reports of a fusty smell associated with the hauntings on the legendary Stocksbridge bypass, but in 1992, as Elizabeth Howard and her boyfriend were driving along the bypass, the car was suddenly engulfed in a very strong smell of pipe tobacco. Neither of the couple smoked and the windows were all closed, so how the smell originated is a mystery.

Smells Fishy

Joe was a devoted husband and was devastated when his wife died. For months he moped around unable to get his life back together but eventually he began accepting the odd invitation from friends and neighbours. Sometimes when the invitation was for dinner or the theatre, he would be paired with a lady and that's when it began – the smell of fish. His friends tried to be polite but they had all noticed, and it seemed to get worse when he was in conversation with a woman. Eventually well-meaning friends decided to take action and persuaded Joe to go to see a clairvoyant. She immediately picked up on the presence of the deceased wife who was making her presence known by the smell of fish. Apparently it was her way of showing her disapproval of Joe getting involved with any other woman.

Other titles published by The History Press

Haunted Derbyshire
JILL ARMITAGE

Drawing on contemporary and historical sources, *Haunted Derbyshire* contains many creepy accounts of spirits, spectres and poltergeists – including the Mad Monk of North Wingfield, the crying angel of Etwell and the headless ghost of Wenley Hill. It also features some of Derbyshire's best-know characters, including Florence Nightingale and George Stephenson, the Railway King.

978 0 7524 4886 2

Ghost Pets & Spirit Animals
JILL ARMITAGE

Ghost enthusiasts and pet lovers can combine their passion in this unique publication which will make a most absorbing read for animal lovers and those interested in the paranormal. With chapters including Can your Pet see Ghosts?, Spectral Horses, Black Dogs and Ghostly Hounds, this book contains many spooky anecdotes and atmospheric photographs.

978 0 7524 3997 6

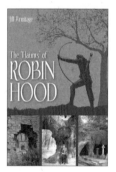

The Haunts of Robin Hood
JILL ARMITAGE

This volume searches for the ghosts of Merrie Men long gone amongst the tree of Sherwood and beyond, through Nottinghamshire, Derbyshire, Yorkshire and into Staffordshire. From hidden caves to ancient abbeys, it discovers the places mentioned in the early ballads and the ancient sites and buildings traditionally associated with this famous legendary figure, as well as something less tangible, but just as real: the ghosts who haunt them.

978 0 7524 4331 7

Romantic Haunts of Derbyshire
JILL ARMITAGE

Since the days of Jane Austen, Derbyshire has been considered one of England's most romantic destinations – but unfortunately not everyone is as lucky in love as Elizabeth Bennet. Containing more than 100 illustrations, this fascinating collection of tales reveal the region's darkest and most tragic love affairs.

978 0 7524 4651 6

Visit our website and discover thousands of other History Press books.
www.thehistorypress.co.uk